David Avrin

More Praise for The Morning Huddle!

"The MORNING HUDDLE is one of the most powerful strategies an organization can practice. It helps drive your culture and engages employees, creating a positive impact on your customers. David Avrin has written a guide that will help make your huddles a success and bring the conversations to life."

—Shep Hyken, Customer Service/Experience Expert and New York Times bestselling author

"Delivering extraordinary customer experiences takes a clear vision, commitment and constant conversation. David Avrin's The MORNING HUDDLE can serve as the catalyst for powerful internal conversations. It will give you the spark, but you have to do the work. Every member of your team has to live a culture of service each day and in everything you do. Grab this book and put those important conversations on the calendar!"

— Dr. Nido Qubein, President, High Point University

"The MORNING HUDDLE is a must read! David Avrin's new book shows you how to invite your customers into conversations that future-proof your relationships and your business."

—AmyK Hutchens, International Award-winning Speaker, Amazon #1 Best-Selling Author and Founder of SheGetsIt.com

"The MORNING HUDDLE creates more of what we need in business — Conversation! David Avrin's provocative new book will push your buttons, challenge your assumptions and kick-start new conversations to solve a new generation of business challenges."

—Joe Calloway, Author of The Leadership Mindset

THE MORNING HUDDLE

THE MORNING HUDDLE

Powerful Customer Experience Conversations
to Wake You Up, Shake You Up, and
Win More Business!

DAVID AVRIN

Copyright 2021 by David Avrin
Classified Press, Castle Rock, Colorado 80108

All rights reserved. No part of this publication may be reproduced transmitted in any form or by any means, electronic or mechanical, including photocopying, recording, or by any information storage and retrieval system, without permission in writing from David Avrin and Classified Press. www.DavidAvrin.com

Reviewers may quote brief passages.

ISBN: 978-0-578-77331-5
Library of Congress-in-Publication Data available upon request.

Cover design by Zain Abideen
Interior by Ajmer Singh
Photo editing by Annie Gough
Author photo by Laurel Wosilius-Avrin

Printed in Canada
10 9 8 7 6 5 4 3 2 1

Dedication

For my remarkable wife Laurel, a gifted listener and patient sounding board, who helps me share wisdom that doesn't suck. Thank you, my love.

ACKNOWLEDGEMENTS

Talking is easy. Writing is hard. Perhaps not for everyone, but it is for me. While ideas seem to flow consistently, focus can be elusive. Look! A squirrel!

The contents offered in this book began as scripts for my video series written over the course of a year. At times, I was excited by a Morning Huddle script idea, while other times I was burdened by the pressure of the deadlines. Through it all, I was able to bounce ideas off my wife, Laurel, who also provided valuable feedback and even an occasional shrug that said: *"Honestly, not your best work."* She provided the voice of the marketplace and helped me to discard what failed to resonate while offering perspective that did.

A big thanks to my brilliant friend Dana Jacobi who suggested leading a Morning Huddle for clients as a way to spur conversation following my presentation to their team. Your idea has changed my business and expanded my thinking about providing ongoing to value to clients, audiences, and fans. I am eternally grateful for your wisdom and encouragement.

A big thanks to CEO group leaders Lonnie Martin and Scott Reeves from Vistage International for agreeing to pilot this series with their CEO members for three months before my launch. It was the weeks and months of feedback that inspired me to revise my content and approach, which has resulted in the powerful lessons I deliver today.

I am also grateful for current subscribers who engage in weekly Morning Huddles around the world in English, Spanish, Hindi, and Mandarin (more languages to come). Receiving notifications that my content is being delivered every week is incredibly gratifying.

A big thanks to my kids (who are no longer kids) Sierra, Sydney, Spencer, Hunter, and Will for your love and support and for being quiet when Dad has to record videos in my studio.

And finally, once again, to my amazing wife Laurel for your endless patience, love, and encouragement. While I burdened you every week for a year, incessantly talking and testing ideas and content (at all hours of the day and night), at the same time, you quietly, diligently, and flawlessly completed your master's degree in Organizational Psychology. You are amazing!

INTRODUCTION
(PLEASE DON'T SKIP THIS.)

There's a great advantage to writing and editing a book during a pandemic. First, you are given the gift of time—whether you want it or not. On the other hand, you have to recognize that you are experiencing an altered reality. The way things are—logistically, behaviorally, and psychologically—will change at some point and the book you are writing has to be relevant and actionable in a post-pandemic world.

The good news is that I didn't write this book for a pandemic. In fact, much of the content was formulated before the world shut down. *The Morning Huddle* is not about the pandemic—although our need to consistently gather, connect, and discuss important issues has been made clearer because of it.

Throughout this book you will notice my conversational tone. This is because these essays began as spoken-word scripts for my popular *Customer Experience Advantage Morning Huddle* video series. But it's also because my approach to business is conversational. This book encourages conversation.

And yes, I start a number of sentences with "and" or "but" because it's how I think and talk. "And" is an acknowledgment that there's often something I need to add in order to clarify or bolster a point. At the same time, "but" allows for a qualifier that offers an alternative perspective that provides additional flavor and insight. My generous use of dashes also provides a frequent aside—because that's how I communicate as well.

If you find yourself overly distracted by my sentence structure, just know that your fixation on the rules of writing will rob you of important messages and lessons. Just sayin'. Oh, and I say "just sayin'" a fair amount as well.

In exploring these subjects, you may not agree with what I have to say. I have no problem with that! This book is about spurring discussion. My intention is not to elicit a chorus of head nodding and guttural utters of agreement. In fact, if everyone agrees with everyone on your team, then your assumptions are not being challenged. In fact, if after having a spirited conversation with your team about an assertion made in this book, you are even more resolute in your opposition to my position on a particular subject, that's great! Now you know why you believe what you believe and are more committed to your policy or behavior. It's who you are, and your customers will come to know what to expect from you.

All of that said, my intention in this book is not to provoke for the sake of provocation. The Morning Huddle conversations are designed to bring important subjects up for conversation and to cause you to think about how you address such dynamics or those scenarios in your business. Where challenges are brought to light, work together to address them. Where new ideas are sparked, discuss how to incorporate creative approaches into your business model.

You can read this book on your own or ask your team to read along with you and then find time—make time to discuss. Ideally, you set aside a specific time each week to gather together, in person or virtually, to discuss a single subject and how it impacts your business and your customers.

You might even be inspired to subscribe and become members of the Morning Huddle video series so that I can deliver the lessons to your team. Information about that is included in the "Working with David Avrin" section at the end of this book.

Finally, ignore what your teachers and parents told you about not writing in a book. Feel free to highlight passages, dog-ear pages, and scribble in the margins! It's not a library book for crying out loud (unless it is). It's *your* book and you should be able to revisit it from time to time, reminding yourself of important lessons when you find yourself struggling with customers or changing markets.

Most importantly, this Customer Experience exploration is not a passive endeavor. Think, discuss, and challenge yourself and each other and each other's assumptions. The world is changing. Your customers are changing and we have to change as well.

Grab a cup of coffee or tea, and let's begin.

David Avrin
President, The Customer Experience Advantage

CONTENTS

Acknowledgements 9
Introduction 11
Divided Attention 17
Being Responsive 22
Stop Saying No 26
Don't Be Hard to Reach 31
Making Us Wait 36
Everything is Personal 40
Competing Against Yourself 43
Someone is Always Watching 47
The Problem With "Fine" 52
The "P" Word 56
Who is Really More Important? 61
Nobody Leaves Unhappy 66
No Second Chances 71
Scheduling Innovation 76
Stop Making Us Do Your Job! 80
Soliciting Feedback 85
Our Favorite Things 90

Throwing Others Under the Bus	94
Real Often Beats Ideal	99
Firing Customers and Clients	104
Your Intelligence Shouldn't be Artificial	109
Your Customers are Telling You More Than You Realize	114
Analogue Thinking in a Digital World	119
Crossing the Conversation Line	124
Creating an Army of Ambassadors	129
The Serendipity Factor	134
The Power of Playing Second Fiddle	139
All They Care About is Price	144
Keep it to Yourself	149
Don't Posture	154
Having a Bad Day	159
Get to Know Me	164
Who's Waiting for You?	169
Happy to See You	174
Convenience Isn't a Store	179
Feeling Cheated	184
Being Remarkable	189
What You Think You Know	194
Cross Train Your People	199
Playing the Long Game	203
One Year from Now	208
About the Author	213

CHAPTER 1
DIVIDED ATTENTION

I know. You're busy. We're all busy. You might even be saying to yourself, *"I don't have time for this today. I have so much to do."* But I need your undivided attention for few minutes, and not your divided attention. Let's talk about why that's so important to your business.

So, you're a multitasker. You take pride in being able to work on multiple projects or issues at the same time. *"Oh, Jennifer is a great multitasker! She rocks. Give her that project, she'll get it done."*

But if you're working on several different things at the same time, are you really able to give anything 100%?

I mean, for things that are task-oriented, like filling out expense reports, or displaying merchandise, or organizing your workspace, being able to spread your focus is not only a good thing, but required of most of us as we go through our workday. We have a lot of demands on our time. However, being adept at dividing your attention shouldn't necessarily be celebrated when it comes to engaging with your customer, clients, patients, constituents, investors, or whoever your audience is. The people you're working to persuade, or impress, or build an authentic business relationship with don't care about all that you've got going on behind the scenes. They might respect it, but they want your attention focused on them—at least during your brief interaction. They want you to focus on *their* questions, problems, or purchase.

Their interaction with you may be brief, but that time is significant for them, because they're handing over their money. Or they're deciding to do so, or have already done so. They want to know that their time is being respected, and the greatest respect we can show our customers is giving them our undivided attention.

> "We can tell when we only have half your attention. We can always tell."

So, how often do you give the people you are working with or working for, you full attention?

We've all had conversations with people who are also glancing at their phone, scanning the room, typing on their computers, or having simultaneous conversations with others while we're trying to talk to them. Some will even look past us to see if there's somebody more interesting or more important behind us or somewhere else in the room. We can tell. We can always tell.

When it comes to your customers or even coworkers feeling acknowledged, important, valued, and heard, anything short of undivided attention makes them feel unimportant, or at least less important, whether or not that was our intention.

For decades, "open door" policies have been celebrated in the workplace. The concept has been embraced with the best of intentions. And while the policy sounds nice, it's rarely effective in actual practice. With a stated "open door" policy, you are essentially inviting people to interrupt you at any time, regardless of the fact that it might take you 10 minutes to refocus on your previous task after they leave. Studies have shown that divided attention rarely creates great work, while focus often does.

When you're working with clients, customers, or coworkers, how often are you also trying to do other things at the same time? What could you do instead, even briefly, to make them feel like the most important person in the room, or on the phone at that moment? We can tell when we only have half your attention. We can always tell.

I've seen young children, fighting for their parent's attention, physically take the cell phone out of their hands, grab their parent's face and turn it toward them as if to say, *"Look at me. Pay attention to me!"*

I used to be that guy. The guy who had a desk full of yellow sticky notes, holding the phone between my neck and shoulder so I could talk hands-free while getting other work done. (I know. I'm old.) But I learned that behavior cost me business and damaged my relationships.

Today, when I get a call from a client and I'm in the middle of something, I'll say: *"Hey, I'm just wrapping something up. Give me 20 seconds, and I'll be able to give you my undivided attention."*

Not only do they always say, "Sure thing," but when I honor that, they are incredibly appreciative.

A more common behavior is trying to finish up what you're doing while after you take the call. Then the person on the other end get's the feeling they're getting only half of your attention as you utter a lot of *"Yeah, uh huhs"*—which is to say you're listening with half an ear.

Which scenario do you think made them feel important and respected?

Friends, this isn't touchy-feely. This is business. Business is built and destroyed on the quality and authenticity of relationships. How people feel about working with you, or working for you, or buying from you, influences their behavior toward you—or toward your company.

There is nothing more fundamental in business relationships than the respect shown during actual engagement. And the best way to show respect is with focus—on their eyes, their words, and an authentic understand of their issues.

The other challenges in your day aren't going anywhere. They'll be waiting for you at the end of that interaction. But we've learned that when those interactions don't go well (from the customer's perspective), the other time-consuming challenges in your business only grow.

My speaker colleague Neen James reminds business audiences that "when you pay attention, attention pays."

Here's why you do it: Most people multitask because they can, and their job requires it. We have so much to do and we rarely have the luxury of doing just one thing at time. I get that. But when we approach engaging with our customer the same way we approach accomplishing our tasks, we're failing to recognize that our customers' feelings about that encounter dictate their actions moving forward. And their actions will make or break your business.

But here's why we hate it: As customers, we don't want to repeat ourselves. We don't want to worry that you didn't get the details right, or truly understand our issue, or got our dinner order correct. When you're looking past us in a conversation at someone else in the room, we wonder what is so important that you keep looking away. When you keep checking your phone, we wonder if you are going to even remember what we've been saying for the last 30 seconds.

Here's a better approach: Gift people your attention. Most encounters are brief. You can focus your attention during that brief exchange or lunch conversation. Everything will be waiting for you at the end. In most cases, that call or text can easily be returned later, and that social media post doesn't need to be commented on anyway. I know. We have a lot to do, but there's a difference between juggling three projects on a deadline and engaging with a client wanting an update on their order. Be aware of all the things that might distract you during a conversation and commit to putting them aside, or at least out of sight for a short time. Lean in. Focus on their face. Listen to the words and don't just wait for your turn to talk.

Giving people our undivided attention is like giving someone a hand-written thank you note. They are appreciated for two reasons:

They are personal, and most people won't take the time to do this for you. Attention is a gift that our customers love to receive. Give it generously.

CHAPTER 2

BEING RESPONSIVE

We often hear about the advantages in business of being proactive rather than reactive. And that makes sense when it comes to having a strategic approach to business. We don't want to have to chase problems, we want to prevent them. But not every scenario is about reacting to or anticipating problems. In fact, there is a third option that's even more powerful and more prevalent.

When I was a kid, we would leave home in the morning and go outside to play with our friends. Sometimes we would come home for lunch, but often we'd just stay out all day riding our bikes, playing in the dirt, or running through the sprinklers at my friend's house.

I'd come home around dinnertime and my mom would ask how my day was and what me and my friends did. The knees of my jeans would get worn through from rough play and I had Band-Aids covering all my cuts and scrapes. There was no GPS tracking. There were no cell phones and no way to reach me directly when I was away. Somehow, we made it through relatively unscathed.

Today's world is very different. Not only can we reach out to anyone, at any time of the day or night, there's also this expectation of a quick response. Think about it. We used to write letters to people and wait for days or even weeks for them to respond.

In the early days of the telephone, if someone didn't answer, we'd just call back later, or someone else would answer the phone for them and take a written message for us on one of those pink note pads. Remember those? Then came the answering machine... and then voicemail. Today, personal electronic devises have changed everything. Not only is outreach instantaneous, but once again the expectation for an immediate response has changed everything.

My 21 year-old daughter goes crazy if I don't text her back immediately. *"Sorry. I was in a meeting."* I'd respond. *"Seriously, chill!"*

On the business side, however, if I don't respond to an inquiry for a possible speaking engagement or a consulting opportunity for a client within an hour, there is a good chance they will have found someone else. That's food off my table.

Everyone has grown impatient with outreach because we have become accustomed to a rapid response, as the mechanisms are in place to facilitate such quick communication.

So, back to proactive and reactive.

We know it's important to be proactive and anticipate customer issues and be reactive in order to respond quickly to issues that arise. But what of those times when there isn't yet a problem, but merely a question, an issue or customer inquiry? How "responsive" are you?

One of the most powerful predictors of business satisfaction is how responsive your customers and clients perceive you to be. You know how frustrated you get when you can't get a call returned or an email or text message goes unanswered. You feel disrespected. Why do you think your customers will feel any differently?

Everyone carries their cell phone with them, which means that people receive emails and text messages within seconds. So, knowing this, your customers wonder why they have to wait for a response from you or your company—*if they get one at all!* They know you got their message!

I recognize that we're all overwhelmed with emails and voicemail messages. Some of us get hundreds of messages a day and it's impossible to keep up. But is it? Really? You know damn well that once an email gets past two days it's likely buried beneath dozens, if not hundreds, of other messages. You aren't going back to find it. You'll forget it's even there.

How many messages per week are you failing to respond to? And finally responding after the sender had to remind you doesn't count. You've already lost credibility and they've lost patience. If you have time to keep your social media updated, you have time to return messages and respond to inquiries.

> *"Customers shouldn't have to remind us to do what we already know that we need to do."*

To be clear, this isn't just about responding eventually. Being responsive is also about answering the phone when it rings! I know you're busy, but answer the phone! Respond to your customers!

I'm not suggesting you have to respond to every spam message or unsolicited sales pitch. I certainly don't. But every legitimate question, inquiry, or request from a customer, a prospect, partner, a fellow employee or vendor deserves a moment of your attention. They are taking the time to reach out. The least you can do is take the time to respond.

The reality is that most in business do a poor job of keeping current with their emails and responding in a timely manner. It's hard, okay? The fact that others are sporadic in responding gives us an opportunity to be strong where others are weak.

Today in business, we need every competitive advantage we can get. Our business success depends on our customers feeling appreciated, respected, and valued. Feeling ignored is counter to all of that. You can do better.

Here's why you do it: Everyone is busy and the number of messages we get per day—every day—can be overwhelming. I get it. Messages get put off and then they're too often forgotten until reminded. But customers shouldn't have to remind us to do what we already know what we need to do. That makes us look unprofessional, or worse, dismissive.

But here's why we hate it: We know you got our messages or emails. Gone are the days of *"Hmmm, I never got your message."* We can see that it was delivered. It doesn't mean it never happens, but really? A legitimate email might go to sp*m occasionally, but text messages all get delivered, and if they don't, you get a notification for that. Honestly, we know that you saw the message and chose to not respond, or you put it off, and that just doesn't feel good.

Here's a better approach: Create systems and expectations in your organization around responsiveness. Just as franchise restaurants might have a policy standard that all food is delivered within three minutes of being plated, you can put in place a policy whereby phones are answered by the third ring. You can decide that all emails are to be responded to within 24 hours or phone messages by the end of day. Responsiveness is either a priority or it's not.

There will always be extraordinary circumstances, but policies, standards, and targets are the only way to assure compliance and consistency. We have to create a culture of extraordinary responsiveness. Word will get out and that will enhance your reputation or brand (which is essentially the same thing).

And remember, it's not about the policy—it's about the people. It's not about the returned call—it's about our customers feeling valued and respected, and nothing is more important than a strong reputation of treating customers well.

CHAPTER 3

STOP SAYING NO

It's been said that the most powerful word in any language is the word "no." We can understand why. "No" can set boundaries. "No" can keep us safe from harm. But when it comes to questions or requests from our customers or clients, too often the word "no" is a too-easy, knee-jerk response that costs you both money and loyalty. Let's explore how to give more consideration to your newly empowered customers.

When you become a parent for the first time, you begin to see the world in a very different way. I'm not really talking about how much your life changes—and it does—but you suddenly see the world as a dangerous place filled with hazards for your child: something dirty on the ground, a sharp object is left out, an electrical outlet within reach, a barbecue grill very hot to the touch.

During those first few years of your child's life, you find yourself saying the word "no" more often than you could have ever imagined. But as our children get older, "no" is more of a barrier between what they want and what they aren't allowed to have, or what we will allow them to do.

"No" becomes the power wielded by the more powerful. This is certainly not a relationship of equals, and it's not meant to be. Of course, being on the receiving end of that restriction is frustrating. When you have a rebellious teenager, generally, they're rebelling against the word "no." And as we grow older and make our way into the world, the power to make our own choices is an added bonus as we become more independent.

So now, when we hear "no," or some version of it as customers, it can make us feel as if our power is being taken away. We are now beholden to someone whose gets to decide whether or not we can have what we want. That loss of power feels bad.

My question for you is this: Do you realize how often you say "no" to your customers or clients? I'll bet it's more often than you think.

Of course, it's not always the word "no" itself, sometimes it's:

"Unfortunately, we don't offer next day delivery."
"Uh, yeah, we don't have anything available till next month."
"Sorry, no menu substitutions."
"Excuse me, sir, but you can't bring your drink in the store."

Now, you may not define that as a "no," but that's what your customers are hearing.

"This is our policy, and it is what it is, and we don't make exceptions for our customers. Yeah, I know you have a unique situation, but we don't really do 'unique.' That would require thinking and making decisions and we kind of have our own rules and ways of doing things."

Of course, sometimes the answer has to be "no."

"Sorry, we can't build you a house in six weeks."

"You're not allowed to bring your emotional support donkey onto the airplane."

"You want roast beef sandwich? This is a vegan restaurant? Yeah. That's a hard no."

But too often we say "no" when we could easily say "yes." Because "no" just seems easier.

We don't want to have to come up with training to accommodate a thousand different scenarios. Honestly, the easiest thing is to just develop a predictable and consistent policy and then have our people do it the way we designed it. This prevents them from having to decide or judge—because they might make a bad decision, or a poor choice, or have to get permission from a supervisor. The easiest answer is just to keep it predictable. Keep it simple.

But in your quest for predictably, you're likely missing a huge opportunity and many potential sales.

The reality is that most requests you'll get in business are pretty reasonable if you stop to think about it. If someone orders a Caesar salad and wants to substitute shrimp for chicken, why not?

> "Most people won't ever ask for a special accommodation, so accommodating the few that do is a smart move."

I know. The cook and the wait staff don't want to deal with special orders. Sigh. Do you know who doesn't care what the cook wants to do? Everyone! Seriously, just charge them a few extra bucks. What's the alternative? Not giving them what they want and then they never come back? Or worse yet, they go online and rant about your poor service? Why on earth would you say "no" to that customer? They're actually sitting in your restaurant! By definition, this is your perfect customer! Why would you not make an effort to accommodate them?

If someone needs an order expedited, there is probably a way to make that happen. Sure, it might take some extra work and creativity, but that's what customers love and appreciate. They feel heard. They feel served and respected, and they learn that they can count on you. If you won't, there is a competitor who surely will.

If we ask for a late checkout at a hotel, it's likely because we need it. (And not everyone does!) When you say "no," or "sorry we can't do that," or quote your policies, we feel unheard, underappreciated. What we really feel is dismissed and disrespected. Buh bye.

Now, the most common argument is also the laziest:

"If we do it for them, we have to do it for everyone."

Not true! That is a cop-out! You only have to do it for the people who ask (if you can). The truth is that most people won't ever ask for a special accommodation, so accommodating the few that do is a smart move.

To be clear, you have every right to design your business the way you want, and to say "no" whenever you want. Just recognize that you'll lose customers because of it—and you may be okay with that. Some hard-to-please customers we don't want, but that will always be the exception.

It is a new world filled with customer choices! Today, there are more and more competitors who will find a way to say "yes" to unique questions and scenarios. When you are inflexible, you'll not only lose that sale, you'll likely lose that customer and the lifetime value of that customer as well. That's a pretty big price to pay for what might have been a simple accommodation that you weren't willing to entertain or offer.

But when you take the time as a team to examine why you say "no" and work to say "yes" more often, you'll discover wonderful ways to please your clients and customers, engender loyalty, and create enthusiastic ambassadors for your brand.

Here's why you do it: You say "no" too often because it's just easier than saying yes—and especially if it's outside of your standard business model. We design our businesses model to create predictability in our customers' journey, buying scenarios, and ultimately revenue for our business. Anything outside of our model is a distraction and certainly much harder to plan for, train for, and quantify.

But here's why we hate it: As customers, we haven't read your employee manual! We don't know *exactly* how we are supposed to do business with you. We just know what we want or need. Our needs aren't all the same, and we want to be treated like human beings. We want to be heard and understood. We want you to empathize with our unique situations, respect our preferences, and the pressures we're under.

Here's a better approach: Where you can, replace your internal policies with reasonable guidelines. Train your people on appropriate decision-making and not just policy quoting. Help them understand what a good decision looks like within the context of your business model and give them more freedom to say "yes" to unique requests or scenarios. That can be scary, but it can also pay huge dividends. Be the hero for your customers instead of just another door shut in their face.

And even when you have to say "no" (and there are plenty of times when you have to) offer an alternative. Say instead: *"Let me tell you what I can do."* Trust me. It's *so* worth it.

When we were kids, we accepted the fact that the word "no" was a big part of our lives. But as adults, we seek out, buy from, and stay with, those who tell us "yes." Just sayin'.

CHAPTER 4

DON'T BE HARD TO REACH

These are amazing times. We have never been more connected to each other and never more accessible—whether we want to be or not. We can call each other, text each other, instant message, DM, Zoom, FaceTime, WhatsApp, and Skype, connect over social media, and more. Some people still have fax machines.

With all of these vehicles and resources available to us, how could it possibly be that some businesses and businesspeople are almost impossible to reach directly? Let's shine on light on this growing problem and very bad strategy.

So, you're looking for a vendor or resource to supply an item, fix a problem, or even just make a dinner reservation. You might go online and look for options. As always, there are many. You call one you've found, but you get a voicemail message: *"We're away from the office..."* Maybe they are out in the field or on the other line, but you don't get a real person and they ask you to leave a message.

Here's the question: Do you leave a message for them? No! Nobody leaves messages anymore. In most cases, we'll just call the next vendor on the list. And even if we do leave a message, we'll call others as well and one of them will answer the phone and very likely be able to meet our needs in some way. In fact, they'll likely seal the deal before others gets a chance to get up to bat.

A sale was lost for no other reason than one answered the phone and the other one didn't.

You'll hear me say this time and time again: The greatest source of lost revenue in your business is the customer that you never knew about!

Of course, there are many other ways that businesses inadvertently, and even intentionally restrict access to real people. Excessively long hold times is the same as being unavailable in the minds of your customers. Worse yet, you are not only *not* available when customers want to talk to you, but you're frustrating them as well. Think about it. You work so hard to attract a new customer or client and just when you have them right where you want them—on the phone or on your website—that's when you frustrate them! Really?

> "The greatest source of lost revenue in your business is the customer that you never knew about!"

It's the most common, yet confusing strategy to save on expenses. Why would you reject revenue as a cost-savings strategy? How many times have you gone to a company website looking to contact someone—anyone— and you can't find a phone number anywhere on the website? We all have. But what do you find instead? Yep. The dreaded "contact form" on the website. Ugh.

If your Web person convinced you to put a contact form on your website instead direct phone numbers, it's time to hire a new Web person! Seriously horrible idea and so bad for your business. People don't want to fill out your contact form. The website contact form is the voicemail of the internet.

I understand why you do it. You want to direct your customers to one central location for inquiries. You want to capture their information for future marketing campaigns. Right? Better still, maybe you can ask some pre-qualifying questions so you can tailor your pitch!

Listen. You have myriad reasons for wanting them to fill out your online form. Here's the problem: They just wanted to talk to someone—and you wouldn't let them! Most prospects will bypass your online form and simply call a competitor. Lost opportunities and lost sales. You may believe it is effective because some people actually do fill out your form, but you have no idea how many people simply click away. Customers almost always want the option of talking to a real person.

And if you think this applies to others and not you, here are a few questions that might make you rethink your innocence. So, in your business:

- Does a real person answer the phone?
- Do you force your customers/clients to navigate your endless voice menu system to find the person or department they're looking for?
- Does your website include phones numbers or email addresses to reach the person or department they want—quickly?
- Do you have work-related, unreturned emails that have been in your mailbox for more than three days? I guarantee that the sender of that unreturned email is feeling ignored and insulted.
- Do your customers and prospects have a way to reach someone at your business or get answers to questions after-hours?
- Are you using a Frequently Asked Questions (FAQ) section on your website as a crutch to save you from being asked the same questions over and over?

Listen, never before has the phrase: "You snooze, you lose" been more relevant in business. There's a lot of snoozin' and losin' going on in the world today. Wake up and grab the business that others are missing.

Here's why you do it: Quite simply, we are striving for efficiency and balance in our business. Managing distractions is a huge challenge and is the one unpredictable part of our day that often takes us off our tasks. Customer calls and requests are sporadic and unpredictable. We have plans for our days. Our employees have things to do and unexpected interruptions from customers or prospects can be both distracting and overwhelming. We have to find a way to manage it.

But here's why we hate it: As customers, we have questions that we want answers to. It's not that complicated. In fact, we know what our problem is, and we have a pretty good idea of how we would like it to be solved. Or, we have a simple question, but it's not a "Frequently Asked Question."

We're pretty confident that our issue can be resolved quickly, or our questions answered, if we can just find an actual person to talk to. You hate it when you can't reach a real person. Why do you think your customers won't?

Here's a better approach: Provide access to as many real people as makes economic sense in your business. And what makes sense has to be weighed against the lost revenue from frustrated customers who leave you.

At the end of virtually every frustratingly long voicemail menu, after the recorded voice has given us nine different department choices, and sub-sub-menus we hear: *"If you'd like to speak with an operator, press "0."*

There it is. After you've exhausted all the other options, online, on the phone, there is a real person available. It just took too long to get there. It shouldn't have. Expectations for access have changed. If others are easier to do business with, they will get the business that you've lost.

The fact that we even have a term for "real people" is almost ludicrous, but there it is. We all want the option of talking to real people. Find a way to help your customers bypass the garbage and get to a real person so they can have an intelligent conversation. Hire them, schedule them, and make them available to your customers.

Often, the increased business revenue and loyalty from your happier customers will more than justify the staffing needed to keep those "real" customers happy, loyal, and coming back!

CHAPTER 5

MAKING US WAIT

What if I told you that you'd have to wait a few hours to explore this chapter's lesson? Would you wait around for it? Not likely. The good news is that you won't have to. It's here and just waiting to explore. Let's dive in.

As I travel the world speaking and working with clients, one of the things I've noticed is that different things bother different people. Of course, a lot of it has to do with our cultural norms or psychological makeup. What may be no big deal to one person is like nails on a chalkboard to another. For example, I hate it when my kids bounce a ball in the house, while my wife hates being the center of attention. We're just different people.

But there is one thing that we can all agree on: We hate to wait in line. In fact, we hate waiting for anything. We hate waiting on hold. We hate waiting for our meals to be served and for things we've ordered on the internet to be delivered. We hate waiting for people to make a decision, for our kids to get ready for school, and we even hate waiting for the microwave oven to finish those last... five... seconds.

So, if you hate to wait, why do you think your customers and clients will be okay with it? As you look at all the points of contact in your business, how many of them are optimized for speed? Speed of response. Speed of answers. Speed of delivery.

To be clear, you can have quality products, phenomenal services, and delicious food, but if your customers have to wait for them, they lose their luster. And if your customers have to wait for what they feel is an unreasonably long time, you are ruining their experience.

One of the primary reasons why people get frustrated by being made to wait is that most often they feel as if the wait was unnecessary. If we wait in line at the grocery store and they have a large number of open, unstaffed checkout lanes, we know that they didn't schedule enough people.

When we have to keep looking at our watch while in a restaurant as others are being brought their food, we feel undervalued or forgotten. When we are waiting for a table and we see a vast number of open tables or an empty section, we are confused as to why we have to wait for a table when so many are available.

If your recording tells us *"We're experiencing an unexpectedly large volume of calls,"* we know you aren't telling the truth. You're not! You know *exactly* when your busy times are, and we wonder why you didn't staff up to better serve your customers.

But the truth is we don't wonder why. We know that you're saving money by cutting staff or reducing hours. We wait so you can save money. To be clear, I'm naïve about business. Everyone has to be smart in terms of managing expenses, but when those cuts directly impact your customers' experience, the "law of diminishing returns" will eventually see our satisfaction give way to our frustration.

Of course, most employees have no direct role in determining staffing levels, but many play a part in delivering services to your customers and clients. Everyone has to be sensitive to those points along your customers' journey where they may be forced to wait for their journey to continue, or wait for answers to their questions, or for their transaction to be completed.

You want customers to love your product, but your process frustrates them. You may deliver wonderfully personalized service, but they were made to wait for what they purchased. And your earnest smile doesn't negate the fact that they were less than thrilled by the experience they received.

We all know that expectations are growing for instant gratification, or at least for expedited gratification. Ironically, the drivers of this shift in expectation don't even need to come from your industry!

People think: *"Well, Uber can show me exactly where the driver is and when they will arrive, why can't you?"*

"Amazon can deliver overnight, why do I have to wait three days for your shipment?"

>
>
> **"If your recording tells us 'We're experiencing an unexpectedly large volume of calls,' we know you aren't telling the truth."**

Call your own business phone number and see if you can recognize how many ridiculous things your customers have to listen to before they get to the menu choice they want. We're asked to enter a number and then have to wait for that number to be read back to us... slowly. Then we are asked if we're willing to take a survey after the call. Then we are asked to listen closely as the menu options have changed. They we have to wait for our choice—if it is even listed. Then we are placed on hold as "calls will be answered in the order they were received..."

I'll bet you're getting frustrated just listening to me recount all of the things you have to listen to. How great would it be if we didn't have to wait to do business with you? What kind of competitive advantage might you enjoy if you were able to reduce all of the times your customers had to wait?

That's not a rhetorical question, by the way.

Here's why you do it: Too often we are on the other side of the transaction. What works for us—works. Too often we fail to see the line of people behind them getting more and more impatient with each passing minute.

But here's why we hate it: The only thing worse than wasting time waiting is feeling like the excessively long wait was unnecessary. We often know in our minds how it could be faster and wonder why you don't recognize it. We hate that you chose to reduce the available staff and your choice cost us our most precious, non-renewable resource: time.

Here's a better approach: Take time to walk your customer's path and recognize where your bottlenecks are. Discover where the wait times can be long and actively and strategically work to reduce them. You have to create the internal flexibility to shift staffing policies and your delivery model when circumstances dictate. Have the flexibility to reassign staff to the phones during busy times. Open another lane. Explore outside vendors for expedited shipping or delivery (there's plenty out there). Go through your online buying process and see if you can reduce the process by a few steps.

Customers vote with their feet, their money, and their time for the companies where they can get what they want, when they want it. Those companies that waste their time, and cost them time, will too often lose their business—in time. Just sayin.'

CHAPTER 6

EVERYTHING IS PERSONAL

At one time or another, we've all heard the assertion that *"It's not personal. It's just business."* But it is personal. Everything is personal!

There's a dangerous and shortsighted dynamic in business of simply dismissing criticism or complaints of what we consider to be "smart" business practices or policies. If something makes economic sense, it's a little easy to let ourselves off the hook by simply asserting that *"It's just business."*

Worse yet is when our customers are made to feel naive or unreasonable for expecting or wanting something that we don't consider reasonable. Implying that if they were just a little smarter, they would recognize a smart business decision. *"This isn't personal,"* you insist—too often in a condescending tone. *"It's just business."*

Give me a break! Of course it's personal! Everything is personal!

Now, you might not intend for it to be taken that way, but if it happens *to* you, then it's personal. You tell us "no" for something we request and think it's reasonable, and we hear *"No. We can't have what we want or need."* We don't see your balance sheet, cost structure, or key performance indicators. We just hear "no," or "sorry," or "we can't," or "we won't." What's more personal than that?

Keep in mind that study after study proves that people buy largely on emotion. We make decisions emotionally and then justify them intellectually. It's not to say that your customers are overly emotional. It just means that we buy for one simple reason: Because we want to. Your job is to make us want to.

You may think that your business policies, procedures, and mandated behaviors are not personal, but your customers disagree. You may think that your clients are being unreasonable, but that disconnect, between what they feel and what you think they should feel, is costing you business—and probably more than you realize.

If something seems screwy to your customers, they will fixate on it. When your frontline staff hears a customer or client sigh loudly during an exchange, that's a good clue they aren't liking you very much. Don't dismiss their dissatisfaction.

"We buy for one simple reason: Because we want to. Your job is to make us want to."

The problem is that you keep following your process and we feel like a number. You keep reading from your script and we feel like we're talking to a wall. You bombard us with survey requests because you need the data, and we begin to regret having ever made a purchase from you in the first place! Yeah, I know. It's just business.

Of course, you're not expected to make poor business decisions, but you do need to recognize that your customers don't always like the decisions you make. You can either shrug it off and risk losing them, or you can work to help them understand why you do what you do. Better yet, you can offer a different scenario, an alternate amenity, or consideration in lieu of what they asked for. Ask them how else you can serve them, and what else might make it right.

People are generally reasonable—so long as they feel heard and respected. Sure, for us it is business, but for our customers, it's not business. It's always personal.

Here's why you do it: We are mired in the day-to-day reality of what it means to run a successful business. There are so many competing forces of customers and staffing, materials, logistics, and regulations. I get it. Business is business, and business is hard.

But here's why we hate it: Your pressures aren't our problem. I'm not being callous. Literally, it's not our problem. We don't work at your business. We just need to buy things and we have no shortage of options available to us. When you are singularly focused on the business side and the economics of what does and doesn't make sense for you, we feel the human side slipping away. Not every scenario is profitable and in business, we may need to be okay with that *if* it engenders loyalty and creates the likelihood of a long-term profitable relationship.

Here's a better approach: Recognize that how our customers feel about us is an important part of the equation. Their feelings don't need to drive every decision, but they have to be taken into account. Truly listen to the feedback you receive, and fix what's broken even if it's only fixed in the mind of your customers (who pay your bills, by the way). If you can't change something, try to explain your process or thinking. Pull back the tent and show them why and why it's ultimately for the benefit of both of you. Offer an alternative scenario, amenity, or accommodation if you can. Most importantly, resist the urge to shrug it off as "just business."

Give people a little credit and they just might give you their business.

CHAPTER 7

COMPETING AGAINST YOURSELF

One of the best ways to ensure that competitors don't steal away your customers is to imagine yourself as your competitor and then trying to compete against yourself. How does that work? Let's explore.

Corporations and foreign governments will often employ computer hackers and challenge them to try to break into their computer systems to see if there are any vulnerabilities they didn't know about. We can do the same thing with our own companies to see if we're vulnerable to others beating us at our own game.

Of course, there are various ways to evaluate our business deficiencies. Companies will hire secret shoppers who pretend to be customers going through the buying process. Then they fill out the questionnaire (that we wrote) and share their findings with us. And while I support any legitimate mechanism that offers insight and feedback from the buyer's perspective, secret shoppers in general have one fatal flaw: They are evaluating the buying experience based on our employees' adherence to their job descriptions and company policies.

Here's the problem: Your customers have no idea what's in your policy manual! They just know whether or not they found the buying experience to be easy, preferable, and if you are easy to do business with.

If you really want to know how to get better, try competing against yourself.

Imagine that you've decided to leave your job at your current company—today. Better still, let's assume that you have secured all the funding you'll need to open a competing company to the one you've just left. You're not bound by any non-compete clause, and you get to take all of your knowledge and experience with you. How would you do things differently?

What if you weren't bound by any legacy systems, policies, procedures, leases, or even staff? You get to start from scratch and serve the industry that you know so well, but based on today's market realities. Understanding that you still have to compete against other players in your space, including your old company, how would you do it?

The truth is that there are companies are out there right now asking that exact question. While you're sitting with your team considering this chapter, discussing your strategies, or just being very good at what you do every day, there are others are out there trying to figure out how to do what you do better, smarter, faster, and more memorably. Let's be clear: Your primary vulnerability is your confidence that the way you do things is the way they should be done. It's not your competitors that you should worry about. It's your complacency.

Take a step back and examine where you are vulnerable. If others can recognize your deficiencies and create an alternate model or revised delivery, so can you! Assume you're that new competitor and look at your current path, policy, or procedures and redesign it. Challenge your thinking and see if you can find a better way. And if you can—do it! Fix it, change it, revise, or enhance it—and do it now. Better you find a better way now than being surprised when a competitor or disruptor does it first and leaves you scrambling to catch up.

The real danger you face is believing your way is *the* way, the best way, or the only way. And not just for the overall customer path but also for each point of contact along their buying journey. Run a little scared every day worried that someone might be nipping at your heels. Because if they aren't already, they will be soon.

> "Let's be clear: your primary vulnerability is your confidence that the way you do things is the way they should be done. It's not your competitors that you should worry about. It's your complacency."

Here's why you do it: We all get a little complacent from time to time because we are good at what we do—both individually and collectively as a company. We are really good at this and our customers and clients like us and reward us with their business. But things change, and they can change quickly.

But here's why we hate it: As customers, we don't really like the old way if we know that there's a new and better way to do something. I don't think we gravitate toward "shiny" objects for the sake of "shiny," but if it is truly better, faster, or more convenient, we turn toward it. Don't let others be the better choice. You should always be working to remain the better choice!

Here's a better approach: The better approach is to run mock scenarios and try competing against yourself on a regular basis. Don't just look at your competitors. Look at your customers as well. Consider all the choices they have and how they like to buy from anyone and everyone in every category.

The world is changing and if you're nimble, if you take a step back and pretend that you're the new market player, you'll recognize your vulnerabilities and have the opportunity to correct them and enhance them before others capitalize on them.

Sometimes a little competition isn't such a bad thing—even when it's just from you.

CHAPTER 8

SOMEONE IS ALWAYS WATCHING

Sometimes, a perfectly fine customer experience can be tainted by witnessing someone else's poor encounter. Let's explore how to recognize those scenarios and how to avoid them.

I think we're all a little voyeuristic. Our ears tend to perk up when we hear a couple arguing, or when we witness an encounter between an unhappy customer and a business owner, clerk, or waitress. Perhaps we just want to see if things are going to escalate, or if we might be needed to help break up a fight.

What I find fascinating is that oftentimes our impression of how our own experience played out is influenced by how we feel others around us were treated during our own customer journey.

In fact, in a 2015 study, researchers observed that when a person witnessed a fellow customer experiencing a "service failure followed by a poor recovery," it significantly lowered their perception of fairness and reduced the chances that they would come back themselves. The study showed that even if the customer was having a good experience, that experience was diminished in the mind of the customer if they witnessed another having a negative experience.

The implications are profound. Not only do we have to ensure that our customers have a positive experience, we also have to be mindful that challenging issues are successfully resolved for someone else or that we handle potentially volatile situations out of public view or earshot.

But I think this goes beyond navigating challenging encounters. We've all been witness to employees gossiping right in front of us, or complaining about working a double shift, or about a "pain in the backside" customer earlier that day, or a frustrating boss or annoying coworker. Do they not know we can hear them—or do they not care?

"We've all been witness to employees gossiping right in front of us. Do they not know we can hear them—or do they not care?"

Back in my 20s (a very long time ago), I received a profound lesson in business that has stayed with me to this day.

I used to sing bass in a popular five-man, doo-wop a cappella group in Denver called The Diners. I have to say that we were pretty good and had an enthusiastic fan base. It was the late 1980s and we would perform weekly at a number of nightclubs in the Denver area but also for a good number of private functions as well.

One weekend, we were hired to sing for a very expensive summer wedding held in a massive tent in the Colorado Mountains outside of Vail.

Our group was set to perform on a small stage at the far end of the tent, with the guests arriving at the opposite end. There was a large no-man's land in between where the dance floor was constructed. For the first hour, the nearest guests were at least forty yards away.

Well, we were young guys and being on our own at our end of the tent, we found ourselves kind of screwing around as we were singing while the guests mingled far away.

Between songs, an older gentleman in a black tuxedo made the long walk across the dance floor and came up to the edge of the stage and motioned for me to lean down. I assumed he had a song request. But instead, he got very close to my ear and said calmly:

"Two things to remember: Number one, someone is always watching, and number two, you're getting paid for this."

With that, he walked backward with his eyes locked on mine, raised an eyebrow, turned and left to join the others.

Honestly, I wanted to throw up—mostly because he was absolutely right, and I was ashamed. It was a profound lesson that I carry with me in business over 25 years later. Someone is always watching.

How conscious are you and your team of what is and is not appropriate to do or discuss in front of your guests, customers, or clients?

Disney theme parks are famous for their delineation of permissible employee behavior. In fact, they don't have employees—they have "cast members." They aren't on duty or off duty. They are either "onstage" or "offstage." Customers are guests. When cast members emerge from the "under park" and join their guests out in the open, they are considered "onstage." It doesn't matter if they are a recognizable costumed character or a maintenance worker, when they are onstage, they are... well, onstage.

If you were onstage in a theatrical production, you would know that any pair of eyes could be on you at any time, and anything you did or said could be viewed or heard.

Business is the same—especially in this age of hypersensitive and aware customers, not to mention the permanence of infractions. Honestly, you have to conduct business today as if every one of your customers or clients is armed with a video camera—because they are.

I'm not suggesting that you shouldn't allow your team to be human or have human moments. We simply have to be more conscious of the eyes and ears that are present. We have to be better. We have to be sensitive to what conversations should happen behind the scenes, or in the break room, rather than in front of our customers. Reinforce to your staff that private conversations, and especially complaining or gossiping, should never occur in front of your customers. We have to find a way to accommodate unhappy customers like never before. It's hard. I get it. But remember that the walls often have ears—and so do your other customers.

Here's why you do it: We're human. Sometimes our dissatisfaction boils over into our conversation, or gossip becomes the default form of communication when work gets a little too frustrating. In addition, not every customer is happy with you and they will let you know that.

But here's why we hate it: We don't want to know that you hate your job. We don't need to know that you hate each other, or worse yet, hate us! We empathize with another customer getting the runaround or facing inflexible policies, because we hate it too! The next thing you know your happy customers are aligning themselves with the frustrated ones who they just saw argue with you. And all of this is a distraction from why we came to you in the first place.

Here's a better approach: Have this discussion with your team. Be very clear what is and is not appropriate to discuss in front of your customers. Remind them that poor encounters with one customer or client is observed by everyone around them. Work to resolve issues quickly, even if you have to swallow hard and just accommodate the unhappy customer. It's often not worth fighting over $10 or $20 bucks if it means saving the relationship or saving face. Remember, it's not just salvaging a relationship with a customer or client, but potentially with many more who are in proximity and aware of the situation.

And like that painful lesson I learned a quarter century ago, in your business someone in always watching, and you're getting paid for this.

CHAPTER 9

THE PROBLEM WITH "FINE"

There's a simple reality in business: Most dissatisfied customers never complain; they just don't come back. Of course, if something goes terribly wrong, you will likely hear about it, as our customers are less reserved today. But what of those who thought you were fine? Just... fine?

"So, how was that new pasta place that just opened up near the mall?" "It was... okay."

"Ok" is the kiss of death in business. Many, if not most in business, deliver exactly what they say they will—efficiently, perhaps even promptly. But if the product doesn't make you glad that you purchased it, if the service didn't add extra convenience to your life, if the food was a little bland, or if the part wasn't easy to install, then everything was just... fine. Not bad—but not great either.

If there were ever a customer or client ripe for the picking, it's the one who was merely served, or sold to. The company didn't do anything wrong, but they didn't do anything great either.

Smart restaurants, for example, will often make it clear that if you don't like the taste of something, they will bring you something else—no charge. To be clear, this is different than not getting your order right, or some other screw-up. This is simply acknowledging that you ordered an item and didn't like the taste.

Now old-school thinking asks: *"Why shouldn't they have to pay for food they ordered? It's not our fault that they didn't like. Everyone else likes it."* Listen, you are well within your rights to stand on principle and let a customer leave unhappy with their selection. I mean, you can't please everyone, right?

The problem is that they will also likely never return. Sure, you made a few dollars profit on the meal, but you also lost years' worth of potential sales from future visits. It's not that they necessarily left mad. They just probably left "underwhelmed." *That*, my friends, is far more dangerous for your business because there are likely many more where they came from.

Okay, so you're probably asking yourself: "Well, if they don't complain (and most won't) how do you even know they were dissatisfied? There are often subtle or even overt clues that are overlooked.

In a restaurant for example, if a diner leaves most of their food on their plate uneaten, there is a pretty good chance they didn't care for the dish. How does the server know for sure? They ask! And when the reluctant diner says: *"No, it's okay. I don't want to be a bother."*

The smart server replies: *"Oh no, please! Let me get you something else. We have some awesome items that are soooo good! Can I give you a few suggestions?"*

"Okay... well, maybe."

If a regular customer hasn't bought from you recently, or you haven't heard from a long-term client for a while, there may be something they are not telling you—or they *are* telling you through their absence. Of course, the only way to know is to ask. You may have to ask more than once if you get a dismissive response or are told. *"No, it's fine."* To be clear, fine is not the same as good.

When I'm traveling to meet with a client or to speak and I drive back to the airport to return my rental car, the Enterprise representative will always say the same thing:

"Welcome back, Mr. Avrin. How was the (insert car model)?"

"It was fine, thank you," I say as I lift my luggage out of the trunk.

"Did you have a chance to fill it up?" they ask.

"No. I was running a bit late. Go ahead and charge me," I admit. And then, they ask me the same question every time:

"Is there anything we could have done to have made this a more outstanding experience for you?"

What they are really saying is: "Please God, don't go on Tripadvisor and trash us for something I can make right, right now."

At the same time, they are also watching your manner for any signs of dissatisfaction so they can intervene, make it right, and retain a customer who was likely hard to win in the first place!

Customers who are "fine" used to simply go away and not come back. Bad enough! Today, too many feel the need, if not the justification, to let their online connections know that you were not the best choice.

"Train your people to recognize the subtle signs of customer dissatisfaction."

In fact, a slew of three-star ratings out of five is far worse than a few one-star ratings. One star says that someone had a very bad encounter. It happens and we get it. But a large number of people who thought you were just "fine" is like being the person on the airplane with a cough. Nobody wants to sit by you.

It's a dynamic that my fellow married guys understand all too well. If your wife is being unusually quiet and you ask if there is anything wrong, and she answers that she's "fine," you know that she's definitely not fine. And now, neither are you.

Here's why you do it: In business, we tend to ignore those that don't complain. They seemed fine. They didn't say anything. We don't want to assume a problem. They ordered and paid. Sounds like a happy customer to me!

But here's why we hate it: Okay, I know this sounds stupid, but people think you just should know if we aren't happy about something. We don't want to have to say it out loud, but we certainly communicate it with body language or an audible sigh. "Whatever," we think. "At least we know not to come here again."

Here's a better approach: Train your people to recognize the subtle signs of customer dissatisfaction. Make an organizational commitment to not let anyone leave unhappy or merely "fine," if you can avoid it.

It is so hard to earn a customer or client the first time. Don't lose future visits or purchases by merely doing what is minimally required of you. Ask, engage, and look for ways to recover in the eyes off your customers.

Caution: Don't "oversurvey" your customers by asking endless questions about their experience. You may feel like you need to, but customers hate it when you're persistent (or relentless).

Remember, customers who are fine are easily lured away by competitors who promise to make them feel pleased. It's a lot better if *you* please them. Just sayin'.

CHAPTER 10

THE "P" WORD

Every year, it seems like there's a slew of new buzzwords that creep their way into our vernacular. Some of them emanate from pop culture. For example, my kids keep using the word *"Woke"* or saying, *"No cap."* Whatever that means. Other terms are thrown around in the business world a little too often like ideate, interface, or growth-hacking. But the dominant word of late is "pivot." Let's explore what is and isn't a pivot, and what's really important to your customers.

Regardless of when you're reading this, there's a persistent assertion made during these tumultuous times about the need to pivot our businesses. Clearly, the world is a profoundly different place than in previous years and we need to make the necessary changes in order to do business differently. The assumption by many is that we collectively need to pivot away from how we used to do things and adopt a new approach altogether.

But do we really need a profound change? Is everything different, or do we merely need to adjust our mindset and continually tweak our approach to respond to changing conditions and altered expectations?

Graeme Codrington, a good friend and brilliant futurist from South Africa, noted that taking your business online, for example, or delivering content virtually, or connecting remotely isn't a pivot. It's merely adopting technology and tools that have been readily available for some time.

In fact, for many, adopting virtual tools to connect with colleagues or customers is actually a case of showing up pretty late for the dance. That shift has been happening for years, and if you've had to scramble to make that pivot in your business, it's only because you were behind the curve—while others were well down that road and likely taking some of your customers with them.

The real question is: What technological advancements, business trends, or societal shifts have you been dragging your feet on adopting? If your business model, your internal processes, or the external delivery of your products or services, were designed more than 15 years ago, your customers and competitors have been leaving you behind.

Think of all that's changed in their lives—in all of our lives that have occurred in recent years. We can buy virtually anything that we can afford from anywhere on the planet from our mobile phone. Most things can be shipped overnight, and anything local can be delivered to your home... today! Information is a mere spoken request away from Siri, Alexa, or Google.

So, your adopting these technologies, or creating a smart phone app to offer greater access, real-time tracking, or ease of ordering for your customers isn't a pivot. It's what's required just to keep up with your competitors and remain relevant to your customers.

A pivot is different. It's a shift in direction. It's a shift in mindset, a significant alteration in our approach to either how we engage with our customers, or perhaps a rethinking of *what* we provide or produce for our customers or clients.

If your market has been profoundly affected or diminished by the coronavirus, or any other reason outside of your control, a pivot asks: What is our core competency? What are we really good at, and who else might need what we can do?

Perhaps we ask: How do we repurpose our machinery, facilities, or workforce to manufacture or deliver something else of value to the marketplace—perhaps a new marketplace altogether. How do we repurpose dormant workers to deliver value in a new and profitable way?

A pivot is when 99% of your customers used to walk into your bank branch at least twice a month to deposit or cash a check, transfer funds, or withdraw money. Now, of course, very few of them do, as we conduct most of our banking on our smart phone or computer. Financial institutions have had to rethink how they forge and foster relationships with their customers and clients. They ask themselves: How do we attract new customers and reinforce customer loyalty when we rarely see them face to face or have the chance to ask them *"So, got any exciting plans for the weekend?"* Our customer experience is now with the app and rarely with the bank teller.

"What technological advancements, business trends, or societal shifts have you been dragging your feet on adopting?"

There's no mistaking it, my friends: The world is changing. Your customers' expectations continue to change at a rapid pace. Their demands for access, speed of service, instantaneous answers to their questions or concerns, and accommodation for their unique scenarios and challenging requests... are changing. The way we avoid having to "pivot" in a significant way is by better anticipating what the world will look like in five years (perhaps less) and doing what we need do to prepared for it.

What minor tweaks to our business model do we need to make right now? What changes are coming next quarter? How will we work and how we will serve our customers next year—and the year after?

If you drag your feet in adopting tried-and-true processes and delivery mechanisms that are common in the broader marketplace, your customers will leave you for competitors. If you fail to listen and respond quickly to requests and complaints about your inflexibility or slow delivery, your customers will leave you for competitors.

A pivot isn't a tweak to your model or mindset. A pivot is a shift from one direction to another, from one approach to another. And while some industries have been profoundly impacted by the pandemic and its aftermath, most companies and their people simply need to be better tuned in and nimble to accommodate the changes that have been happening for some time.

Listen. Adapt. Adopt what is already available and often widely used by others and that your customers come to expect and appreciate. You probably don't need to change everything, but you do have to change as your customers change.

Here's why you do it: We too often see tumultuous times and changing markets as a crisis. It's a big deal in our mind, because change is hard and scary. We've worked hard to create and refine a business model that's smart, effective, and predictable. Provided we have enough customers, this model works and we're really good at what we do. It works and we don't know if changing will work as well.

But here's why we hate it: Our world has changed. It's changing all the time. When you cling to your long-standing model, mindset, or approach, we see you as stagnant or antiquated. When you scramble to pivot (and you're likely just catching up to competitors) we wonder what took you so long to offer that convenience or amenity. You think you deserve a pat on the back, while at the same time we're being enticed by competitors who just moved past you... again.

Here's a better approach: Recognize that a pivot, by its very nature is reactive. We're changing in response to something that has impacted our business. We're playing catch up or looking for a different approach when responding to a negative occurrence or unexpected competition.

The better approach is to proactively challenge your own business mindset and approach before something external impacts you again. Know that the way you do things isn't necessarily the way things need to be done. It's merely the way you do it—and it probably has been for some time.

If we make the act of questioning our assumptions and shifting and revising our model and approach an ongoing endeavor, we will be far less likely to need to make a profound pivot in the future.

Keep in mind that if you launch a new website or debut a smartphone app for your business, you haven't gained some amazing new competitive advantage. Honestly, you've likely just caught up to the marketplace. You didn't pivot. You just stopped falling behind... for now.

Stay nimble. Keep enhancing and revising your model and approach. Never stop listening to your customers. Trust me. They'll tell you what they want. In fact, they already are.

CHAPTER 11

WHO IS REALLY MORE IMPORTANT?

It is certainly *en vogue* to tout the importance of an employee-centric culture. I would suggest that perhaps the pendulum has swung a bit too far. Fair warning: This is going to be a bit of a rant and you're more than welcome to disagree. Regardless, the conversation is important.

I saw a meme posted on social media espousing a popular assertion, one that is often repeated by well-meaning company leaders and "culture" consultants because it sounds really deep and insightful. It's often attributed to Sir Richard Branson, but to others as well.

"Our employees are more important than our customers. It's very simple: If we treat our employees well, they will treat our customers well."

You've got to be kidding, right? That about as pithy as: *"Everything you want in life is on the other side of fear."* Oh, that's so deep! Go embroider it on a pillow. Most of what you want is on the other side of hard work, and you know that.

To assert that our employees are more important to our business than our paying customers sends the wrong message to our team. To assume that they will know how to best serve your complicated customers merely because they have been treated well by you is naive.

Our focus needs to be outward—to serve and please our paying customers and clients. Our customers are the most important thing—albeit in a long list of very important things that also includes: our employees, business ethics, cost structure, logistics, supply chain, profitability, jobsite safety, and much more.

But our paying customers are at the top of that list. They are the sole reason we exist and the only reason we get a paycheck. Our customers pay the bills, and this may shock your sensibilities, but our employees *are* the bills.

"Do you know what makes employees really happy? Keeping their jobs and getting paid fairly for the work that they do. That only happens when we are consistently profitable."

I've seen very happy employees be less than accommodating with customers. By the same token, I've seen others feeling real pressure from their supervisors to deliver a knock-it-out-of-the-park performance. I'm not advocating the harder approach for staff, but I am dispelling the myth of predictable cause-and-effect service. Happy employees = great service. Not necessarily.

To be clear, culture is indeed paramount! But it is a culture of service, accommodation, empathy, and doing what it takes to be the best choice for our customers and clients that translates into business success. The profitable culture is an outward-focused, service-minded one where the satisfaction of customers takes precedent over the preferences of our employees.

I'm not suggesting that it is one or the other, or that they are mutually exclusive. A great work environment is a powerful thing and great for employee recruitment and retention. But when accommodating employee preference takes the focus away from your customers' journey, you have lost the point of commerce. When your policies and procedures are designed to make life great for your team but make the buying process less convenient for your customers, you are losing the battle.

The landscape is littered with Silicon Valley startups that envisioned themselves to be the "coolest" place to work, with personal chefs, flexible working hours, and volleyball courts, that now sit vacant because they didn't have enough paying customers. D'oh!

When was the last time you heard someone rave about how great it is to work for Disney or Amazon? But you often hear about their legendary customer-focused culture! Shareholders don't clamor for monthly "culture reports." They expect to see earnings.

Our policies and procedures are not crafted to make life great for our team but to make doing business remarkably easy for your customers. We're not necessarily sacrificing one for the other, but certainly catering to one over the other.

Do you know which companies survive and thrive? The ones with a lot of paying customers. In fact, they are the only companies that survive. Of course, some have great cultures, while others have cutthroat cultures. To be clear, I'm a big fan of a great internal culture where employees are valued! It's easier to recruit and retain great people. Culture is crucial, but it's a customer-focused culture that gives your organizations its competitive advantage and the best chance for profitability.

Of course, not every customer is worth saving. There are a rare few that we are certainly better off without and we have to protect our staff from abuse. But as a rule, everything we do is ultimately designed to make life great for our customer—to make us the better choice in a growing sea of great choices. Your culture should be focused on delighting your customers, making their life easier, getting them what they need faster than others, and providing a buying experience that they want to share with their tribe.

Do you know what makes employees really happy? Keeping their jobs and getting paid fairly for the work that they do. That only happens when we are consistently profitable. Not marginally profitable, mind you. Not sporadically profitable. Consistently and profoundly profitable. Profoundly profitable companies expand and hire more people and pay those people every month.

We need to pull back the curtain and demonstrate to our team how we make money. We need to remind them that our survival, and that of their job, is predicated on being remarkably easy to do business with, on happy customers who come back again and again and tell others of their great experience. When we do that better than others, we have a successful and profitable business that will be around next year.

Here's why you do it: We certainly want to do right by our people. We want to be the boss that we always wished we had early in our career. Attracting and retaining great people is hard, and great, happy employees are incredibly important. Without employees, we have no business. Well... yes and no.

But here's why we hate it: It sounds good in practice, but the facts are daunting. The vast majority of businesses fail, and they don't fail because of a lack of happy employees. They close their doors because of a lack of business. Both are important to be sure, but we live or die on revenue, cash flow and profit.

Here's a better approach: Talk to your team constantly. Reinforce why we are here. Pull back the curtains and explain your numbers. Be honest and transparent about what it takes to be profitable. How many paying customers are buying what items or services at what price and how often? What is the lifetime value of a customer? Then look at all the other choices those customers have. Talk about what we have to do to be a better choice, to serve our customers at a higher level, and to be astonishingly easy to do business with.

Only then—armed with this information, clear job descriptions, your mentoring, leadership, and encouragement—can your employees make your customers happy.

Please don't misinterpret my point. Your employees are incredibly important, and the best ones know why they were hired and what our customers expect of us. Let's turn that original assertion on its head:

"*Our customers are the most important thing to our business. It's very simple: The more happy customers we have, the more happy employees we can have!*

Now that's a meme to share on social media!

CHAPTER 12

NOBODY LEAVES UNHAPPY

Despite our best efforts, some customers and clients will get angry. Sometimes they're mad at us and sometimes at our process. They'll even get frustrated at things that are completely out of our control. But often our success is dependent on our ability to take back control of those situations and de-escalate unfortunate situations. Let's explore the importance of nipping these scenarios in the bud.

In a previous chapter, we discussed customers who were... fine. Just kind of "so-so" about us, and how dangerous that can be for your business. But what of those customers or partners or vendors who aren't fine? In fact, they're not happy at all. There is something they don't particularly like, or worse yet, something they're angry about.

Perhaps they're frustrated by a late delivery, an excessively long hold time, a rude employee, or just the fact that they aren't getting whatever they want—their way. There's no shortage of scenarios that can cause any of us to get a little miffed. It could be a process, a company, or even an individual.

The question is: Do your people know how to respond in those instances? Better still, do they know why it's so crucial to the future of our business that nobody leaves unhappy—if we can help it?

We hear a lot about the power in commerce shifting to the consumer. In most cases, they're referring to the fact that consumers have more information at their fingertips than ever before. They have the power to research on their own, compare vendors, and ultimately to choose whom they wish to buy from. Business success today is less about how we sell and more about how they buy. There is less of a reliance on salespeople to educate us prior to a purchase decision. The easy access to information about features and benefits has empowered our customers.

But there is another aspect to the idea of "consumer power" that's far more dangerous for you and your business. The fact is that unhappy customers can hurt us in very tangible and substantial ways. Frustrated, angry, unreasonable ones can be relentless in their desire to harm our business.

> "Unhappy customers today don't just take their business elsewhere, they take their dissatisfaction online."

Consumers are more and more weaponizing review sites like Yelp, Glassdoor, and Tripadvisor. Online communities can conspire to destroy a movie by coming together to post negative reviews on Rotten Tomatoes—even before the movie comes out! Do these sites have too much power? In a word: absolutely! But that's the reality we have to live with today, and to be honest, our competitors have to deal with it as well. The worst part about the power of the Internet and online review sites is that there is no "truth test" to the content being posted and we have little to no power over their policies. But make no mistake, we have great influence over the people who might post negative reviews.

We can work harder to give them a more positive experience and mitigate the negative ones. We can solve their problems, address their concerns, and fix what's broken before they "go rogue" on us. We can work harder to accommodate their special requests, bend our policies, and even fall on our sword when needed to de-escalate a situation gone wrong.

Does this mean we can solve every problem or make everyone happy? Of course not. But acknowledging that doesn't absolve us of the obligation to do what we can for those situations we can handle better.

The old adage that *"the customer is always right"* is the right mindset, if not overly simplistic and often impractical. However, it is a good, concise way of saying to our staff that we need to be of service to our customers and not try to be right—even if we are. If there's a disagreement and we become overly zealous in our attempt to make clear to our customers that we are in the right, we may win a battle, but we will ultimately lose the war. Swallow your pride and keep the customer happy.

It's been said that most unhappy customer don't complain—they just don't come back. Unhappy customers today don't just take their business elsewhere, they take their dissatisfaction online—and those negative comments or rants are permanent.

Instead of teaching your team that the customer is always right, a better assertion would be more like:

We have to defer to customers whenever possible. Our survival depends on our customers getting what they want, when they want, and delivered to them in the way they prefer it. If they choose others to make a purchase, we lose. If they leave us for competitors, we lose. If they are unhappy with something and we can't make it right or reduce their frustration, we lose.

Are customers more demanding than in previous years? Sure. Are clients getting more impatient? Absolutely! Can they be threatening at times? Oh yeah... *and?*

Here's the point: You need to sit with your team and discuss the top things that your customers or clients request that you felt the need to say "no" to. Review the reasons why your customers become frustrated and talk about all the potential responses you have at your disposal. Ask yourselves, how far are we willing to go to be of service to our customer and ensure that they don't leave unhappy?

The good news is that most of your customers are happy—that's why they are your customers!

I know how hard it is to "give in" when the other person is wrong or being insulting. Just keep in mind that this isn't a conversation among equals. This isn't a fight with your 12-year-old sibling, or your parents, or even a friend. We are conditioned our entire lives to stand up for ourselves, to make our case, and win arguments. But in business, we have to relearn and rewire our brains. We must change our perspective when it comes to interacting with our customers.

Remember that this is an interaction between you and the person you hope will spend money with you, and not tell others that they don't like you. It's not a normal interaction. It's not.

Would you rather be right or be effective? Be right or struggle for years to overcome negative reviews? Be right or be profitable? You already know the answer to that question.

Here's why you do it: We have a business to run. If people are asking for unreasonable things, or if they're unhappy with something that might not even be our fault, what are we supposed to do? If we do it for them, we have to do it for everyone and then we go out of business!

But here's why we hate it: Bogus argument! You don't have to do anything for everyone. Everyone doesn't need what we need, nor are they embroiled in this contentious situation. We know that you could easily do something to make this right. We think you're just being stubborn and unreasonable and don't care about me or earning my business. You know what? I'm going to make sure everyone knows how I was treated today!

Here's a better approach: Breathe and think. When you're in an uncomfortable scenario, even where you know you're right, resist the urge to stand on principal. I know how hard it is to swallow your pride or bite your tongue when a customer is being unreasonable. Don't take it personally. The goal is not to win the argument but to lower the temperature and end the conflict.

Ask yourself and ask your customer: *"What would it take to make this right?"* If their response isn't doable, try to meet the customer in the middle or offer an alternative: *"Let me tell you what I can do."*

Just do something... for them. Even if they don't get everything they want, often it's their perception of whether you tried to make it right or how reasonable you were that will determine what they feel about their experience with you and, more importantly, what they do after they leave.

CHAPTER 13

NO SECOND CHANCES

One reason, in a long list of reasons, why we need to get it right the first time with our customers is an interesting dynamic that has become more common in recent years. Let's discuss.

A notable casualty of the widespread availability of quality products and services today is the death of the second chance.

In yesteryear, if we had a mediocre experience with a business, we would just shrug it off and figure they were having a bad day and perhaps it would be better next time around. At the next opportunity we'd simply try a different menu item or trust that we'd have a different person across the counter or on the other end of the phone. No big deal. Today, it's often easier to just choose a competitor rather than take the chance on another less-than-expected experience. Today, we rarely give second chances.

We move on for two primary reasons. First, we become fearful that the second experience won't be any better than the first. We think, *"What would lead me to believe that it would be better next time around?"* We're just not going to spend time wondering. Instead, we shop from a different vendor next time. It's not like it's going to be hard finding someone else to meet our needs and take our money.

The other reason we easily leave a business or vendor is more personal. We don't like feeling slighted or we were bothered that you didn't care enough to give us your best. Worse still, if we felt mistreated or ripped-off by receiving minimal value for the price we paid, we take it personally. We feel as if we were disrespected, and we don't respond well to being disrespected. We paid but didn't get what we asked for. We made an appointment, and you didn't show up. We paid for expedited delivery, and it arrived late. See ya!

Of course, most people are reluctant to complain or confront a business, so they don't. But there is a danger in mistaking our silence for complacency. We aren't okay with it and we'll likely just vote with our feet. We will grace you with our absence simply out of a personal feeling that you don't deserve a second chance. You let us down and we refuse to reward that behavior or pretend it didn't happen.

> "It's not that customer loyalty is dead, it's just much harder to earn and sustain today because it's become so easy to leave you."

Now, this might sound a little petty and not very understanding, but the truth is that people can be petty and not very understanding. If we feel underserved or disrespected, we don't want to reward your poor behavior with our business. In most cases, it's not even that conscious on our part.

They say that the opposite of love isn't hate—it's indifference. We don't hate you if you underperform a bit on the first go-around. We don't know you or care about you enough to hate you. We just don't come back.

Most won't even take the time to rant about you online. They just won't come back. If we spend our money on you and we don't feel we got appropriate value for our money, or that you failed to live up our expectations at any point along our journey, and if you didn't make a legitimate attempt to make it right, we just won't come back.

If you don't show up when you said you would, we likely won't reschedule; we just write you off. When you advertise a delicious meal and it fails to impress, we move on. When you promise big results and then under-deliver, we consider it lessoned learned and we end the contract. There are countless competitors standing in line. We're not being unkind or even trying to punish you in most cases. We're just very cognizant of all the options available to us.

In a 2016 global consumer survey conducted by the artificial intelligence company, (24)7.ai, 47% of those responding said they would take their business to a competitor within a day of receiving poor customer service and nearly 80% said they would do it the same week!

Of course, those numbers don't necessarily apply to your long-standing customers or clients, but we can't take them for granted either. When you have a relationship with a client, you'll often get another chance if things don't go well. But even in those circumstances, there is a real danger if your relationship is largely transactional. If it's something we can easily buy elsewhere, you're at great risk if something goes awry.

It's not that customer loyalty is dead, it's just much harder to earn and sustain today because it's become so easy to leave you.

That's why cell phone companies want to lock you up in a service contract. They know that most customers would be gone in a flash at the first sign of frustration because their customer service is so lousy. So, instead of concentrating on doing a better job of addressing concerns and staffing their technical support lines appropriately, they make sure that you can't leave them—at least for a couple of years.

The truth is that most of us have only one shot to deliver for our customers. We spend a lot of time, money, and creativity trying to attract new customers. But to get that in-person opportunity with a new customer or client and blow it due to a service failure is inexcusable!

Of course, we can't always know if a customer is a first-time customer or a longstanding one, but should that even matter? Our employees have to be very clear that the long-term viability and sustainability of our business is dependent upon the long-term patronage of our customers. Remember, you can't have a repeat customer until they become a first-time customer. And they have to want to come back. They have to! You may have gone through your system or processed your transaction thousands of times, but for many of our customers, it's their first time and they are judging you on your performance. You have to be up to the task each and every time.

Here's why you do it: Too often, our focus is on the customer-acquisition portion of the relationship, rather than the excellent delivery of the services itself. The truth is that it's often what happens *after* we get the customer that determines whether or not we hold on to that customer, and it's hard not falling into a routine. *"I know what I'm doing,"* you say to yourself. *"I've done this a thousand times and I can do this with my eyes closed."*

But here's why we hate it: We don't want you to do it with your eyes closed. We want you to open your eyes and see us. Try harder and let us know that you respect our decision to give you our money. Don't do it half-heartedly or with a face that says *"Ugh. These customers are so exhausting."* Seriously. I'm giving you a chance to earn my business. Don't just offer it. Earn it!

Here's a better approach: Recognize that customers today have limited patience or tolerance for underperformance. Make a commitment to rise to meet their needs and expectations and not just your job description. Not everyone will, and that's your real opportunity to gain market share from others who blow it.

Say what you'll do and do what you say. It's sounds basic, but at the very least you have kept your promise. Keep your head up, keep your eye on the ball, and any other metaphor that you need to hang your hat on to make sure that each engagement with every customer is as if it's their first time—because it just might be!

It's no different for your competitors. You likely have only one chance to make a great impression. Don't blow it.

CHAPTER 14

SCHEDULING INNOVATION

We speak a great deal about examining your customers' journey to identify points of friction. But there is a danger in focusing most of your efforts on what *not* to do. Read on as we discuss a unique strategy for out-innovating your competitors.

As parents, we're often reminded to "catch our kids doing something right for a change." We get so focused on steering them in the right direction as we help them navigate their early years, that it's hard not to focus on everything they do wrong. All parents know that our kids are often doing things they're not supposed to do—or at least not what we wish they would do.

The danger is that we can find ourselves always looking for what's wrong, while they're left feeling as if they can't do anything right. We don't want to raise children who are so worried about missteps that they never stray from the path. Sure, they might comply out of fear of punishment or ridicule, but they'll also lack the courage to try new things, be adventurous, and step out of their comfort zone. That's where life can be great!

The same holds true for our employees. We want them to be compliant to be sure, but also be sensitive to our customers' needs. We want them to be smart, but also to be creative and look for ways to improve our processes and enhance our customer's journey.

The danger in "playing defense" is that we direct so much of our attention to making sure that we don't do anything wrong, that we miss out on opportunities to go beyond the script and consider ways to delight our customers and clients.

"Put creativity on the calendar!"

Of course, the terms "customers" or "clients" may not apply to everyone on your team, but everyone has an audience or constituency. For some, they may serve other departments within your organization, while others deal with vendors, partners, investors, suppliers, users, and more.

So, whomever you serve in your role, after eliminating points of friction or frustration for those you deal with, revisit their journey and look for ways to make it more memorable, unexpectedly easy, expedited, more personal, and ultimately, more promotable.

During World War II, Lockheed compiled a team to work on a top-secret project designing the P-80 Shooting Star fighter plane for the US Air Force. This elite team was given wide discretion to work outside of the normal company structure to come up with something different, something revolutionary. The "Skunkworks" team worked offsite, outside of the main building to provide a measure of secrecy and to remove the walls that surrounded the other workers.

Today, the Skunkworks philosophy has been adopted by some of the best companies in the world. Well-known technology companies use the model for top-secret projects where an elite team can work in secrecy and without traditional management oversight. But all companies can reap the benefit of the Skunkworks mindset by taking days off the calendar to allow their people the freedom to explore redesigning products, reconsidering points of contact, and turning processes on its head.

Here's a great exercise:

Give your people a "magic wand" and ask the question: If you had no constraints on technology, resources, or even budget, what would you do to change your job, or redesign our offering to help clients love us more? What one new thing could we do, offer, or provide that would bring a smile to our customers and cause them to talk about us and boast about their experience? There are no dumb ideas and no expectation that what is created by the team will come to pass.

Where do you think great ideas come from? We all get busy doing our job each day and there's often little time to turn off our duties and turn on our creativity.

Put creativity on the calendar! It can be part of the Morning Huddle membership initiative I launched, or it can perhaps be a single day each month dedicated to creativity. Stagger your teams so that everyone has not only the time, but also the mandate to look for ways to make their customers' journey better, faster, easier, and more worthy of sharing.

Consider all the ideas and decide which ones are far-fetched, which items are things we probably should be doing any way, and others which could become game-changers in our category. What would it take to bring that new idea into practice in our company? What resources would it take and who should be involved? How much time would it take and what would be the impact on our customers, our brand, and our revenue?

The best ideas from the likes of Apple, Google, Boeing, Microsoft, and others come from Skunkworks projects. Your best ideas and new amenities and products can come from your own people, if you give them the freedom to create, ideate, and collaborate.

Here's why you do it: We focus on doing what we're supposed to do, the way we're supposed to do it, because we are looking for predictability and consistency. If everyone does their job, that's the best way to keep the ship pointed forward.

But here's why we hate it: What's often lost in the quest for consistently "good" is the potential for "excellent." Like our kids, we all need the opportunity to grow and stretch and be recognized for doing something great and innovative—and not just cautioned against what we're not supposed to do.

Here's a better approach: Introduce a Skunkworks mindset, if not the actual structure into the mix—perhaps on their own or as teams. Give your people both the mandate and the freedom to create, solve and envision something new and perhaps better. Take the time to focus on a single point of contact and envision a new and different way of delivering your service or engaging with your customers. Run scenarios, and then re-run them.

Fix the problems in your customer's path before their dissatisfaction costs you their business. But also look for ways to do what you do more creatively, more memorably, and with more promotability. It just might earn you a greater measure of their loyalty.

CHAPTER 15

STOP MAKING US DO YOUR JOB!

It seems more and more these days that many of the shopping experiences are controlled by your consumer. And while having do-it-yourself options and choosing our own buying journey can be very empowering for consumers, not all such options are welcome.

Many of us remember that scene in the movie *Back to the Future* where Marty McFly is walking around his town square in the 1950s. As he looks across the street, he sees a car pulling into the gas station as it is immediately "attacked" by four gas station attendants. One immediately begins washing the car's windshield, another starts checking the air pressure in the tires, someone else is pumping the gas, and another lifts the hood and checks the oil—all of this while the family sits comfortably in their car. For my kids, this scene might have looked like a NASCAR pit stop, but this was a good depiction of life in the 1950s and '60s. It was commonplace.

Of course, today there's only one option that isn't really an option. If you want gas, get out of your car in the snow or rain and pump it yourself.

Now, is it really a big deal to have to pump your own gas? No. In fact, most people don't remember it any other way. But this permanent shift to a do-it-yourself model for filling up your tank is really just reflective of so many tasks that have been pushed on customers.

Today, after shopping for our groceries, we go through self-checkout, scan each item at the machine ourselves, pay the machine, bag our items ourselves, only to be stopped by the exit to have our receipt checked to make sure we didn't steal anything.

Then we push the shopping cart out to the car and load the bags into the back. With the exception of the shopping itself, every one of those tasks used to be performed by a store employee. Of course, today many of us can have our groceries delivered, though it is not yet an option for everyone. These new delivery options notwithstanding, the point is still valid. We are in a do-everything-for-yourself world.

Think about all things that used to be done for us. It's not that we were lazier back then, it's that businesses just worked harder to compete for our business.

Of course, some of the do-it-yourself advancements are welcome. We love doing our banking on our cell phone or withdrawing cash from an ATM. It's super-fast and we don't have to drive all the way to the bank—during banking hours! We love avoiding the hassle of having to take time off work to go to traffic court to pay our parking fines when we can do so online.

But it's the mundane tasks that begin to grate on us. If I have a grocery cart filled to overflowing, I don't want to be encouraged to use the self-checkout line. What will likely take me 20 minutes, with a lot of frustration for every item that doesn't scan right, a trained checker-outer could do in five. Why should I have to scan a cart full of groceries? I don't work here. You do!

I'm not trying to be demeaning. To the contrary. I honor you. You're really good at this. You have done it a thousand times. I don't want to learn your job. I have a job. I'm paying you to do it.

When I go out to dinner at a restaurant, I'm not washing the dishes afterward. If I were going to do that, I would've cooked my own dinner and eaten at home. That's why I am paying you do it.

At the airport, I don't want to tag my own luggage. I'd rather just wheel my luggage over to the trained professional to put the tags on for me.

Mostly because I really, really need my luggage to be waiting for me at the end of the trip. I don't want to screw it up!

To that end, doctor, you go ahead and cut the umbilical cord attached to my newborn baby. You're the one who went to medical school! I'll just run the video camera and pretend to be my wife's breathing "helper."

> "This is how a free-market economy works. We will buy from you as long as we are satisfied. When we're no longer satisfied, or inconvenienced, we will go and buy from someone else."

You may think I am being elitist, but I assure you I'm not. I'm just busy and don't want my purchases and buying journey delayed as I try to learn someone else's job. I expect the businesses I choose to do their part. If they will do theirs, then I will do mine. By the way, my part is to give them my business and spend my money with them. If they fail to do their part effectively, or cause me more hassles, then I will take my business elsewhere.

This is how a free-market economy works. We will buy from you as long as we are satisfied. When we're no longer satisfied, or inconvenienced, we will go and buy from someone else.

Voicemail is the same. Apparently, we've now been hired as your receptionist or HR staffer. After listening to an endless menu (that probably doesn't include our destination) we have to figure out for ourselves where to find what we need. That call, if answered by a knowledgeable person, could direct our call to the correct person or department in mere seconds.

Instead, the job of navigating your complex organizational structure has been shifted to us because the cost savings of eliminating these gatekeepers was too alluring to resist. as your new gatekeeper, I'm still waiting for my W2 in the mail.

It's also clear that many companies will do anything to not answer our questions, so we get directed to an FAQs or chatbots. (Bot is short for robot, incidentally.) They make us scan and search and figure it out for ourselves when they could have very easily answered it for us. Oh, but they're *so* tired of answering the same questions from their customers about their business. I totally get it.

Now, it would be easy to simply accuse me of whining about my "first world" problems or complaining about minor inconveniences—but you would be missing the point and the missing opportunity. This is about a competitive marketplace and the battle for customers and clients. If burdening our customers with a growing list of inconveniences is becoming the norm, then there is a great opportunity to buck the trend and once again do for your customers and clients what others no longer provide.

While a competitor may point to the far end of the store, directing customers to retrieve their own requested item, you can personally take them there instead. When others push you to the Frequently Asked Questions (FAQ) section on their website, you can give them an easy-to-find phone number and a real person to answer their specific question.

What's lost every time another activity is shifted to your customers is the good will and positive feelings necessary to forge and retain beneficial customer relationships. When you work so hard to build a business, create products, refine services, deliver excellence, and attract customers only to overburden those you so desperately want to impress, well, that's on you.

> **Here's why you do it:** The primary reason that you shift activities and responsibilities to your customers is to lower your staffing costs and remain price competitive. I get it. By and large, ongoing expense reduction is a wise move and a smart strategy.
>
> What's the big deal? All of your competitors are doing it. It seems pretty basic.

But here's why we hate it: Because it adds up. It's just one more inconvenience, especially if we are in a hurry. We think, *"You work in this business every day. You have the experience. Why am I having to do your job? I have a job!"*

Here's a better approach: Always look for efficiency in your business, but if reducing tasks for your employees requires transferring them to your customers who have a choice of who to buy from, then it's probably a bad idea and likely costing you more than you are saving!

Resist the urge to follow the pack. Call them trends, shifts or even disruptions if you want, but that doesn't make them good or right. Hold off as long as you can or buck the trend and even reintroduce what others have eliminated. If there is a needed service task, then do it for you customers—and do it cheerfully! *"Here, let me get that for you!"* Your customers will recognize it, appreciate it, and reward you for it.

Keep doing your job and your customers will likely keep giving you their business.

CHAPTER 16

SOLICITING FEEDBACK

So, how're you doing? I'm seriously asking. How are you doing? Are your customers and clients happy with you? Are you sure? There are good ways and bad ways to learn the answers to those questions. Let's explore them.

In yesteryear, organizational leaders were reluctant to bother their customers with surveys or requests for feedback. Honestly, if thing were going well, there was no need to rock the boat and certainly no reason to place doubt in the minds of our customers by giving them a list of things they might not have realized they were unhappy with.

Then there was that very scary question we didn't want to ask our longtime customers: *"Why do you keep doing business with us?"* The fear is that some might think: *"Hmm. Why do we still buy from them? Hey, O'Brien, let's put this contract out to bid!"*

Even in the workplace, leaders are often reluctant to ask their direct reports for feedback, fearing that the comments might be less than flattering—and who wants to hear that?

Today, of course, the world is different. We are inundated with requests for feedback from merchants. Verbal requests, email requests, website pop-up requests, being asked to hold after your call to take a short survey. Even the checker at the grocery store spending a few seconds circling something at the end of the receipt and letting us know that if we call this number and take their survey, we can be entered into a drawing for... something.

Or worse yet, we're calling our doctor and after finally navigating through the endless and unnecessary options, we have to listen to another message and hit a number on the phone to let them know that we don't want to take the survey. I just want to reach my doctor. Stop burdening me with this frustrating process that serves your needs but ignores mine and delays my care!

> "I understand your need for information. Just make sure that your aggressive tactics don't diminish our impressions of the buying experience."

It's getting overwhelming, and ironically, it's damaging the very customer experience and perceptions that the company is trying to better understand.

So, what's driving this seemingly desperate quest for feedback? There are a few reasons: At the most basic level, it's the need for simple feedback to gauge the satisfaction of customers. Of course, shortsighted organizations do little to nothing with the information they get. It's like the suggestion box we used to see in the company break room in yesteryear. You wondered if anyone ever even read those suggestions.

Some of this actually goes back to the days of the comment card stuck between the salt and pepper shakers on restaurant tables. The real purpose of those cards was to capture your information for future marketing. It was like, "Give us your feedback and sign up for our birthday club!"

One of the reasons for the immediate survey request after your purchase today is to gather psychographic information about your likes and dislikes, what you bought and why. They want to maximize their marketing efforts and tailor future sales pitches to fit your wants and needs and preferences. Generally, a smart move.

The main reason, however, for the request for feedback is to find out if you were dissatisfied with some part of your customer journey. If you return a low score or a negative comment, smart companies have a process in place to make sure that someone reaches out to you quickly to find out what happened and see what needs to be done to make it right.

The risk of unhappy customers floating out there can result in both the loss of future sales—pretty painful for your business—as well as a dissatisfied customer leaving a negative review online. Both are important issues that can be brought to light through the survey.

Here's the problem: We generally don't want to take time to fill out your survey or answer your question. We came to you to make a purchase or meet a need and we have done so. We've moved on to whatever else we've got going on in our life.

Does this mean you shouldn't ask for feedback? Of course not. Just don't make it bothersome and don't ask more than once. Seriously. If we didn't fill out your survey, it's not because we forgot to and we don't need to be reminded. It's because we didn't want to. Stop asking.

And when your survey is programmed in a way whereby multiple reminders are sent if we fail to respond, the positive experience we had with you has now been tragically transformed into a poor experience. We likely would have bought from you again, but you made us so uncomfortable with your relentless requests for feedback, that we have become frustrated with you. Understandable intentions—but with predictable consequences.

Can you imagine if that person holding the clipboard who approaches us at the mall kept following us as we tried to politely wave them off? Every time we looked up as we were shopping, they were right there in our face, asking us again to fill out their survey. Well, if you send out multiple reminders asking for feedback, that creepy person is you.

We have all been a victim of this. In an effort to make sure we had a great experience, they diminish that experience by the relentless asking for feedback. Do you see the irony here?

Some of the most effective feedback techniques involve simple, single, open-ended questions that allows for honest feedback *at the point of purchase*, while also allowing a worker to address an issue before the patron actually leaves.

For example: As I recalled in Chapter 9, after a returning your car to Enterprise, the workers ask: *"Is there anything we could have to have made this a more outstanding experience?"* We have an opportunity at that point to let they know if there was a problem with the car, if the satellite radio didn't work, or even just to reaffirm that everything was great—also important feedback.

A waiter or waitress will stop by the table and ask: *"Is everything to your liking? Was the food prepared properly?"* Even if I was reluctant to motion them over before, they are now right there and asking a specific question.

"Well, since you asked, I don't want to make a fuss, but I asked for no onions on this and it's hard to pick around them." The waitress offers a heartfelt apology and rushes to make it right.

It didn't take any more time out of my day. I didn't have to navigate an online form. She didn't have to ask me twice, and better still, she was given the opportunity to rectify the situation before I left unhappy.

To be clear, I am not anti-survey, but most of us are becoming overwhelmed by how often we're asked to fill one out. My guess is that you are too.

Here's why you do it: We need to know how we're doing. Our survival is predicated on happy customers, on our best customers, and clients coming back again and again. And while we think we have a good handle on how you feel, we do need the data.

But here's why we hate it: It's just too much. Maybe not from you, but it all adds up, and honestly, we've just learned to tune it out. We are asked for our feedback by most vendors after most purchases. Do you really want to be thrown in that bucket as an annoying company and a relentless stalker? That last-touch impression doesn't support the brand you're trying to build.

Here's a better approach: Consider ways to get the feedback you need, but in a less obtrusive manner. Ask at the point of purchase something specific about their encounter. If you have an actual survey, don't send it after every purchase or inquiry. Communicate with us how short your feedback survey is (and yes, you should make it short). And if you want a better sampling of your customers, offer them something of value in exchange for their comments, feedback, or suggestions. I understand your need for information. Just make sure that your aggressive tactics don't diminish our impressions of the buying experience.

CHAPTER 17
OUR FAVORITE THINGS

We all have our favorites. I'm not talking about your kids, but your favorite restaurant, or car, clothing brand, television program, mobile phone, or coffee shop. So, what do our favorite things, or favorite businesses have in common? More importantly, what can we learn from them?

When I grew up in Denver, Colorado, in the 1960s and '70s, there was this family restaurant called The Denver Drumstick that was my favorite place to eat. In fact, it was every kid's favorite place. It was a simple, sit-down, family restaurant, but they had this electric train that traveled from room to room on a ledge built about a foot below the ceiling.

The restaurant was divided into several different rooms, and as you ate dinner, every few minutes you could hear the train coming! Eventually, it would appear through a hole in the wall, travel around the perimeter of that dining room and then disappear again though a hole in the opposite wall about 30 seconds later.

It's so funny to think back at how much we anticipated that little train coming back into our room as we'd watch it go along the wall and then disappear again. Then we would all turn back to our delicious chicken dinner. I was thinking about it the other day and sort of wondering: What was it that made that place so special? Why did I ask my parents to go to The Denver Drumstick every year for my birthday dinner?

In thinking back, I realize that it wasn't just one thing. It was combination of things. It was the memory of how much fun I had the last time, and it never disappointed. It was the community of all the other families with kids my age there for the exact same reasons: great food and great fun. We all loved the little elevated train. We saw our friends and neighbors. It was that shared experience with people like us.

Over 50 year later, I recognize that it was also the consistency and predictability. There was never a night that the train wasn't running. They didn't overwhelm us with an ever-changing menu trying to cater to every possible taste. It was fried chicken with a specialty of serving drumsticks: chicken with a built-in handle for kids to hold and all served in a little cardboard train box. It was so cool!

It was also the buzz. Everyone knew the place, loved it, and all the kids talked about it. Now, granted, the simplicity of an electric train would likely struggle to keep the attention of todays' kids, but it was appropriately fun and unique for its time.

The point is that The Denver Drumstick knew their audience and they catered to them—and only them. They didn't try to be all things to all people. They focused on being the best choice for their target market: families with young children. The food, the atmosphere, the price point, the amenities, and even the informal entertainment was geared toward pleasing children and their parents who got to be heroes for bringing them there.

Now, does this mean that single people, or childless couples, or even grandparents wouldn't also enjoy the experience? Not at all. But it certainly wasn't designed for them. Any attempt to modify the product or the experience to accommodate or impress all those other demographics would have likely diminished some aspect of the experience for their core audience.

If they tried to attract more single people, families would notice fewer people like them. If they expanded the menu, it would have been less fun to see meals being served just like every other restaurant.

The point is that you have to know your audience. Know who these people are, the other choices they have, why they buy, and why they don't.

Gear everything in your customers' journey to be seen as the best choice for your best customers.

Of course, we are happy to serve others, as their revenue is just as valuable to our business, but understand that we aren't designing the products or experience for them. We are delivering it for everyone, but we are designing it for our core audience.

> "When you try to be acceptable to everyone, you won't be exceptional to anyone."

Think of the businesses you return to again and again. I'll bet in most cases the reasons are not really top-of-mind. You just know that you like the fit of their clothes, the atmosphere of that restaurant or the ruggedness of that truck. It feels like... you.

But if you look closer, you'll also likely find that they get you. You'll find your tribe: others who share your unique fashion sense, taste for comfort food, or your passion for outdoor adventures.

When others like you gravitate toward a company, product, or even an experience, there's good chance that there is a conscious targeting strategy behind it. That's what smart businesses do.

Take a step back from your company and your role and get clear on who your ideal clients or customers are. Not everyone who buys from you, but who is *most likely* to buy from you—if you do things right.

Think of all the things that your target market would love from a vendor in your space. Keep in mind that what a couple in their 70s might love will likely differ from that of a young couple in their 20s. There's nothing wrong with that. Just know your target, decide who you will focus on, and deliver to them consistently, uniquely, and preferably every single day and in every single transaction.

Don't worry about the masses. Pick a lane. As they say: There are riches in niches.

Here's why you do it: We are so worried about leaving money on the table that we try to make sure that we have something for everyone. What happens too often is that we become a good choice for a lot of different groups but certainly not special or preferable to any of them.

But here's why we hate it: Okay, we don't really hate generalists, but we don't love them either. Being really good isn't special anymore—especially when others are working hard at targeting a segment of the population and knocking their socks off!

Here's a better approach: Focus on your target market and cater to them. Grab a piece of paper and create a list of your favorite companies and break them up into several different categories. Write down just one company per category and then list the things you love about them. See if you notice any common themes emerging. More importantly, ask yourself if your customers feel those things about you and your company. Then list and discuss what it would take to engender those feelings and loyalty from your target customers.

Remember, to be successful, to see growth, you have to be a good choice for most everyone, but a really great choice for your target market.

As I like to say, when you try to be acceptable to everyone, you won't be exceptional to anyone.

CHAPTER 18

THROWING OTHERS UNDER THE BUS

How often do you throw others under the bus? We certainly don't want to take the blame for something that wasn't our fault, but we all tend to shift the blame a little too often—and probably more often than you think. Let's discuss why we need to eliminate this far-too-common behavior.

So, a delivery is delayed, a size is wrong, a meal gets mixed-up, or an order arrives incomplete. Things happen, but you are the one that gets the call or finds yourself face-to-face with the frustrated customer or impatient client. Your first responsibility, of course, is to tell the customer what happened.

"I'm so sorry. The shipping department keeps screwing this up."

Or *"The kitchen is a little overwhelmed and some of the meals are going to the wrong table. This keeps happening. I am really sorry!"*

Or *"Someone in the warehouse grabbed a different item by mistake. I'm really sorry."*

You tell the customer that you understand how frustrated they must be (as we've all been trained to say) and set about to fix the problem. Seems like a logical and appropriate way to handle the situation, right? Not necessarily.

Anytime we shift the blame (even it was their fault) what we're really saying is: *"It wasn't my fault. Don't blame me."* Of course, we get to be the hero for fixing the problem, but we've also diminished our company and denigrated our brand in the process.

When we ascribe blame, we don't look like a team. We don't look like we have each other's back. We look like we're all out for ourselves and trying to save face.

Realize that in this moment all of this is now about you, and none of this is about the customer. But, of course, it's the customer who has the problem that needs to be solved. Seriously folks, get your ego out of it.

Lest you think I am immune to this damaging behavior, I too have found myself succumbing to this "easy out." Allow me to explain.

I used to lead CEO roundtable groups for Vistage International (the world's leading CEO organization). I had an open seat in my group and was evaluating a new prospect looking to join my CEO roundtable. I'll call him "Mike." This was our third meeting, and we had a really good fit. In fact, I assumed he was going to sign the agreement and join our group when we met later that day.

So, I arrived for our scheduled meeting, and after entering his office, he greeted me and then closed the door behind me.

Mike sat behind his desk and started explaining that he had been struggling a bit that week with a staff problem. He found out that his customer service employees and billing department employees were "bad mouthing" each other. Worse yet, they were complaining about the other in conversations with customers.

He explained that when a customer called with a complaint about their bill, or the service that had been provided, a staffer from the billing department would say that the customer service department had clearly dropped the ball. Or the customer service would throw billing under the bus by blaming them for whatever the problem was. He was struggling with how best to confront the situation and change the behavior.

So, Mike turns to me and says: *"Then I got this voicemail message last Friday,"* and he turned to the phone on his desk, hit the speakerphone Button, and began to dial. To my surprise, the voice on the recording was mine.

"Hi Mike. This is David Avrin and yes, you are correct, the meeting place listed in the e-mail invitation for our next group meeting was wrong. Some 'bone-head' from the corporate office listed the wrong location."

Then, without ever taking his eyes off of me, Mike pressed a button on the phone rewinding it slightly. Then he hit "play" once again.

"Some bone-head from the corporate office..."
Click.
"Some bone-head from the corporate office..."
Click.
"Some bone-head from the corporate office..."

I sat speechless as Mike leaned back in his chair. After a brief pause, looked at me and began:

"So, here's my dilemma, Dave. I'm looking for an executive coach to help me become a better leader and deal with issues such as how to confront poor internal behavior, and this message is what I received from my leading candidate. What do I do with this?"

All I could do was nod knowingly, acknowledging that everything he was saying was true and the concern he was sharing was richly deserved. I screwed up—big time. Not just because my poorly considered, off-hand comment had violated my relationship with a valued corporate partner that I represented, but because I had damaged my credibility with someone I had great respect for and was hoping to earn his respect in return. It was careless and no one's fault but my own.

In that moment, I knew the worst thing I could do was to offer an excuse or try to talk around the massive "elephant" sitting in the middle of the room. Instead, I acknowledged what we both knew to be true. I screwed up. I offered my sincere apology and told him that he was right to call me out on my poor behavior and that I knew that it had damaged my credibility.

Now, as I flash back to my frustrated state at the moment when I had left that recording, I realize that my remarks were simply a poorly considered, knee-jerk reaction (emphasis on "jerk") to a situation that I feared would damage his perception of me and our organization.

A wrong location had been listed in an email. It happens. Instead, it was *my* actions that diminished our credibility. So, once again, all I could do was apologize.

By the way, Mike ultimately did join a CEO roundtable group—just not mine.

"*In most cases, it's irrelevant to the customer who was to blame, so why even go there?*"

Any of us can fall into the trap of shifting or ascribing blame, whether or not it's deserved.

To be clear, I'm not suggesting that we should lie to customers as to who was to blame for a mishap or mistake. I'm saying that in most cases it's irrelevant to the customer who was to blame, so why even go there? They just want to know that their concerns are being heard and the problem will be corrected. They need to know that we will take the necessary steps to make sure it doesn't happen to them again. Fault is a distraction to expedited resolution.

Don't throw your coworkers under the bus. Just get in the driver's seat and steer the bus back in the right direction so we can all arrive successfully together.

Here's why you do it: I think it goes all the way back to our childhood. When our brother or sister did something wrong, sometimes punishment from mom or dad was swift and harsh. We think: *"I'm not taking the blame for something I didn't do!"* But in business, we have to resist the urge to deflect. Worry less about blame and more about helping your customers get their problem resolved.

But here's why we hate it: As customers, we don't care who did what. Seriously. We don't care if your hands are clean. We just want the issue resolved, the order delivered, the call returned, or the part to fit right. Your shifting blame just makes more of your company look bad and we're already frustrated!

Here's a better approach: Worry about what went wrong *after* you address the problem. We do have to make sure that we document and correct issues so they don't become recurring problems, but that's out of sight of your customers and should be handled *after* we get our customers what they need.

At the end of the day, things happen. People get that. We just don't want to make the situation worse by further reducing their perception of our competency by making others on our team look bad for what is often just an honest mistake.

Telling the truth isn't always the best policy when the truth is irrelevant. Focus on the solution and let our coworkers retain their dignity and help your company retain its reputation.

CHAPTER 19

REAL OFTEN BEATS IDEAL

We are all bombarded with ads, social media posts, and other imagery touting the ideal face or physical form, the perfect life, and the allure of wealth and excess. But let's be honest, 99% of us are nowhere near perfect! I want to discuss the real buying power of real people.

No matter how much we pretend to not care, the grass always seems greener on the other side of the street. We often want what we don't have, and marketer recognize this. The quest for perfection—in all aspects of our lives—fuels massive industries around the world.

The beauty industry pitching skin care, hair care, makeup, perfumes, toiletries, and deodorants, surpassed $90 billion in the USA in 2020 and will account for over $800 billion globally within the next three years. That's nearly a trillion dollars just trying to live up to how others tell us we should appear and present ourselves physically.

While you certainly don't need me to tell you that this quest for perfection drives a lot of revenue, most of us also recognize that we'll never be perfect. Few people will ever be successful supermodels, social media influencers, or Hollywood A-listers. That said, we can certainly try to be the best we can be.

The problem with trying to keep up with the Joneses (as we say in America) is that we rarely feel good about ourselves in the process. We're fat-shamed about our weight, we feel "less than" if we can't buy our kids everything that their friends have, or they see celebrity influencers flash around online.

Most people aren't rich or famous, or beautiful, or muscular. It's not that we shouldn't aspire to better our circumstances or ourselves, it's that we also need to recognize that there are far more of us than there are of them.

And as much as I tout the importance in business of finding that unique segment of the population to serve, recognizing that there are "riches in niches," sometimes the best niche is actually the wider population. While we all have our unique demographics, needs, desires, and even idiosyncrasies, there are some broad threads that also bind us together.

One of the smartest business models in the world is the one created by Planet Fitness. Most fitness-based companies (nutrition, clothing, fitness centers) feature healthy, fit, and beautiful models demonstrating the equipment, wearing the clothes and drinking the protein shakes. Planet Fitness by comparison, employs a totally different approach. It's less about aspiration and more about inclusion.

They call their gyms "No Judgement Zones." In an early Planet Fitness center, the word "judgement" was accidentally misspelled, but they didn't fix it, because they are a "no-judgment zone!" Now they misspell it on purpose in many of their location. In fact, they have over 2,000 fitness centers with more than 15 million members—and they are just getting started.

The key to their success is that they are unapologetic about their focus on real people.

The membership prices are cheap, and they don't offer steam rooms, aromatherapy, or high-end spa amenities. That said, they have a modern, functional locker room with showers and lockers. The clubs are clean, well run, offer unlimited tanning and massage chairs (for a small premium), and rows and rows of workout equipment. As a direct response to Covid-19 concerns, they've even expanded to offer online workouts for members.

What they lack in margin, they make up for in volume. And even for those that tend to fall short on their workout resolutions, it doesn't even make sense to drop the membership because the monthly dues are so cheap.

As a result, their member retention is far above industry averages. What you don't see at Planet Fitness is many body builders with tank tops, people carrying jugs of water, or fitness models parading around in an endless fashion show.

"Not everyone is looking for the ideal. Sometimes, good-enough at a better price point, is a better choice."

What you do see is a real people wearing T-shirts and gym shorts working hard to stay healthy. There are a lot of them because there are a lot of us! The experience is friendly, welcoming, non-threatening, and non-judgmental. Members know why they are there, and they share the appreciation of not having to be onstage for others to judge their bodies or stamina. (Those concerns are what keep millions from exercising in public).

Members even wipe down the equipment themselves, for crying out loud, because they have that much respect for other real people who are just trying to get their workout in. That, my friends, is commonality. That is community and a shared experience of imperfection that's propelling Planet Fitness to astonishing new heights.

And yes, I am a member. And no, they don't pay me to endorse them. In fact, I pay *them* for the privilege of lifting heavy things and sweating with others like me.

Others have recognized the value of targeting the masses as well. The term Volkswagen literally means "people's car." There are certainly awesome high-end and specialty niches automobile options available around the world, but Volkswagen had the intention of creating a car for the average man and the average woman. Low price, low margin, but they made it up in volume. Volkswagen's niche was the masses.

So, while you focus on your core market, think also about what binds the broader market together. What's the common denominator?

I learned this when teaching my son fractions in math. Stay with me on this. He was being asked to add 2/3rds and 4/5ths. I told him: Imagine that you had to add two zebras and four giraffes. You can't. You have to find a common denominator. What do they have in common? They're both African animals! Two zebras and four giraffes equal six African animals.

Dove soap, for example, features real, imperfect people (like most of us). Smash Burger recognizes that most people love a great big sloppy burger with cheese and bacon, and IKEA has built a juggernaut selling inexpensive items to real people in settings that demonstrate what it would look like in a real-world small apartment or office or kitchen.

Find what's common among the broader populations that you serve and see how you can attract more of them by including them and focusing on what they have, need, and like together.

Here's why you do it: We tend to fall into two camps: We either try to be all things to all people and end up being seen as a "generalist," or we target a specific category and go all in as a "specialist." It's a tried-and-true formula, so why experiment?

But here's why we hate it: Despite our very polarized world right now, there is more that connects us than divides us. We aren't always in our own camps, especially when it comes to purchasing. Aspirational marketing is a proven strategy but it can also leave us feeling a bit insecure when we know we can't live up to the ideal.

Here's a better approach: Consider a contrarian strategy of appealing to a broader market. Don't ditch what works but look to see if there is also room for a more inclusive approach.

Not everyone is looking for the ideal. Sometimes, "good enough" at a better price point is a better choice. Some of the most loyal customers simply appreciate not having to be perfect. They are good, honest, hard-working people doing the best they can. Just like the rest of us.

CHAPTER 20

FIRING CUSTOMERS AND CLIENTS

Many of us have been fired from a job at one time or another. It was likely as a teenager for a bad attitude or doing something stupid. (Maybe that's just me.) But if companies can fire their employees, can't we also fire our customers? There are times when that might be the only reasonable course of action. Let's take a look.

By and large, business owners and managers have the right to decide who does and does not get to work for them. I'm not talking about the freedom to violate employment or discrimination laws, but in general, employers choose their employees. The hires that work out get to stay and continue to receive a paycheck as long as they fulfill their job requirements. The ones who fail to perform sufficiently are given the opportunity to work somewhere else.

But what about customers who don't work out? I mean, if we can choose our employees, shouldn't we also be able to choose who we agree to sell to? (Let's not go down the discrimination road. That's not what I'm talking about.) Can we not decide which business relationships to invest in, nurture, and prioritize?

Of course, we can't always choose who buys *from* us. We can choose our target market and work to convince them that we are a good choice, but ultimately, they get to choose where to spend their money.

But sometimes business relationships can sour. Just as in our personal lives, either party can choose to opt-out of a romantic relationship. *"It's not you. It's me,"* we say trying to soften the blow. Of course, we are really saying: *"It's you. I'm just not that into you anymore and I'd like to break it off."*

In business, however, it's much less about our feelings. More often, feeling the need to end a business relationship is about recognizing acceptable or unacceptable behavior, demands, or expectations. To be fair, we put up with a lot to make a sale and retain a customer. We smile and work to serve customers regardless of their attitude or the day we are having. And if they do their part—which is to pay us for our time, our products, expertise, services, and more—then we work hard to hold on to that business relationship.

"Most unhappy customers don't want to be placated. They want to be accommodated."

But when their poor behavior or unreasonable demands tip the scales to such an extent that we begin to question whether this relationship is even worth it, it's time to take a pause.

So, what kind of scenarios or behaviors might drive you to that tipping point?

Of course, if scenarios involve violence or threats of harm, that's a hard stop. If law enforcement is needed, then it's pretty clear that the relationship has come to an end. But other more common dynamics often involve customers or clients who simply refuse to be satisfied or placated. No matter what you do, no matter how hard you try, or how accommodating you are, they are just going to be dissatisfied and demand more and more. At some point, you just have to walk away.

The real challenge for those of us in business is to know when we've reached that point of no return. In yesteryear, you could pretty much wash your hands of a bothersome customer or client whenever you wanted to.

"Ya know, I think we're done here," you'd say. "You've rejected a very good paint job three times and I've already lost enough on this deal. I'm done."

Today, we have to weigh the frustration and revenue loss we suffer when trying to placate an unreasonable customer, with the damage they could inflict upon as they vent their frustrations online.

When a customer has become frustrated (for any number of reasons) we've been trained to use empathetic phrases like: *"I know how frustrating that must have been."* Or *"I'm so sorry that this happened, Ms. Jackson."*

To be honest, I think most people have grown tired of that script because every business utilizes it. The words are almost robotic at this point. They want you to give them what they want. Then again, some just want to win.

So, when you've exhausted every plausible scenario, and offered them everything within reason, you've swallowed your pride, and already lost any potential for making a profit, and they still want more, it may be time to walk away.

But how do you end the relationship without creating the bigger problem of a rogue customer hellbent on exacting revenge? The truth is that most unhappy customers don't want to be placated. They want to be accommodated.

First of all, *you* need to be the grown-up in the room. I'm not suggesting that you treat them like a child, but you need to seek the higher ground, take control of the narrative, and lay out the proposed conditions for the relationship exit.

As they are likely in a triggered state, we first have to remind them of everything that we have done to this point to accommodate them or make the situation right.

"Mr. Stephens, let me remind you of how we got to this point... When you asked for blank, we delivered blank. And when you weren't satisfied and *requested additional blank, again we gave you that modification. I'm not sure there is any scenario that is going to get you what you want."*

Resist the urge to say "you." *You* did this, or *you* are unreasonable... Use a "we" statement: *"We* feel that... *We* have tried to..." *We* believe that it's important to..."

Now, here is the important part: Before you break off the relationship, give them *one last thing*.

Perhaps it's some extra portion of what they were asking for in the first place, or something else that *they* value, to show that you are not simply standing your ground but being extraordinarily accommodating. *"So, here's what we're willing to do Mr. Stephens: We are going to give you blank, or credit you back for the blank. And at this point, I think it's best for both of us that we move on."*

What you've done is ended the unhealthy relationship, but in a way that has taken away their ammunition and defused their animosity toward you to some extent. They're still walking away (which is good for both of you) but likely doing so with less anger or a measure of resignation. Perhaps they even felt like they've won, and we have to be okay with that.

You don't want unreasonable customers to walk away angry. You just want them to walk away.

Here's why you do it: Historically, the point at which a business relationship no longer is orth continuing was determined by whether or not it remained profitable. Today, it's far more complicated, as our customers, or former customers, have a powerful bullhorn and a platform to do us harm. We have to approach the dissolution of that relationship very differently.

But here's why we hate it: There are few things worse than giving in to an unreasonable customer or those who believe they can bully us by threatening our business with negative online reviews.

Why should we give in to outrageous demands or offer things that would lose us money? Are you kidding?

Here's a better approach: You have to ask yourself *"How much is it worth to make this person go away? How much better would our life be if we weren't having to deal with this distraction, or abuse, or have to overcome negative online reviews?"* As much as we might want to fight, remember that you have far more to lose than they do. Swallow your pride, take a breath and resolve the situation.

If you have to walk away, offer them a "parting gift" to help diffuse the situation. Even if you feel you've given enough already, offer them one last thing that *they would value* and then agree to part company.

Listen, every business relationship ends at some point. Most often it's the customer who decides when to walk away, but sometimes our sanity requires us to let bad customers go and end the relationship.

"It's not you. It's me. I need to be rid of you. And here's a lovely parting gift!"

CHAPTER 21

YOUR INTELLIGENCE SHOULDN'T BE ARTIFICIAL

There is a lot of talk these days about Artificial Intelligence (A.I.) and how it promises to enhance the customers' experience. And while the prospects of a more predictive engagement and interaction can be enticing for business, we have to be careful when eliminating true human empathy and creativity from the mix. Then again, there is also a risk in our customer conversations mimicking A.I. rather than A.I. mimicking us.

A generation ago, futurists depicted A.I. with images of humanoid looking robots working side by side with real people in cities of the future. Today we see fast moving robotic arms and shooting sparks as autonomous machines weld car parts together on an automotive assembly line.

The most common use for A.I. today is utilizing "big data" to better understand our customers, predict their behavior and anticipate questions. When specific, relevant ads are directed to you online, it's because data about your previous searches and purchases were collected. Then, tailored marketing messages were delivered to you.

And while some may find that creepy, it's a smart approach. I personally appreciate not being inundated with ads for feminine hygiene products, vegan dishes, or hunting gear. They're not bad. They just have no relevance for me, so why should companies pay to deliver ads to me that are unlikely to result in a sale? Big data help business avoid wasting money.

The most common direct interface between humans and artificial intelligence today is through online chat features. In case you hadn't figured it out by now, most chat features are "staffed" by chatbots—and "bot" is short for robot.

> "It's bad enough that we can't get the chatbots to think and understand the unique nature our question, but when we feel unheard by actual people, our frustration grows and grows."

What chatbot technology companies are doing to the best of their abilities (and it is getting better all the time) is anticipating nearly every possible question you might ask, worded in countless different ways, and then offering pre-programmed responses. And whenever the chatbot asks *"Did that answer your question?"* and you click "yes" or "no," it gets smarter. It actually learns. That's "I" in A.I. and what distinguishes A.I. from a regular computer program.

Perhaps it's just me, but chatbots rarely seem to have the answer to the question that I'm asking. Then it just keeps repeating the answer it *wants* to give to me over and over. To be fair, I'm often asking the same question over and over, just hoping it has a feature that recognizes frustration and defaults to a real person redirect.

But how often do we find ourselves in similar scenarios involving real people, perhaps in retail, or with a customer service rep, or on the phone with technical support? No matter what we ask, they just quote their policy, almost robotically, again and again. You know they have a script in front of them and they just tell us what they're supposed to say *regardless of what you trying to explain to them or ask!*

When people say, *"It felt like I was talking to a brick wall"* this is what they're referring to.

Let's assume, for argument's sake, that we're hiring intelligent people. If they aren't free to use their brain or deviate from their script to address our actual questions or concerns, they come across as "artificial" and that's really frustrating for your customers.

It's bad enough that we can't get the chatbots to think and understand the unique nature our question, but when we feel unheard by actual people, our frustration grows and grows.

This robotic behavior is most often a byproduct of the fear of our employees deviating from the predicted and prepared-for scenarios and into the unknown. We tell them to just stick to the script or the policy. Because if our staff is free to do what they want, say what they want, or offer what they want, they why do we even have a business plan or policies? It's just going to devolve into anarchy! So instead, we tend to over-script our responses. But if you do that, your people become nothing more than a human FAQ.

Just as no two of your customers are exactly alike, so too are the issues or questions they have. We expect the chatbot to get it wrong fairly often, but we don't want humans to not hear us, or fail to truly understand the issues we're trying articulate.

If you want some specifics, here are some examples of common internal behavior that adds too much "artificial" to your human engagement:

Scripted empathy:

"I know how frustrated you must be, Ms. Carter."

Listen, I do agree that we need to show compassion, or at least empathy for what they're going through, but these statements all sound artificial. My advice is to always think about what your parents or close friend might say. Real empathy sounds more like:

"Absolutely! I want you to know that I hear you, Ms. Carter. I've been there myself. The good news is that I'm not going to leave you hanging. I will stay with you until we get this taken care of."

It's conversational and it's authentic.

The second behavior that screams "artificial" is the repetition of responses. Too often we think our customer just doesn't understand our answer, or they weren't listing, so we repeat our policy. In reality they completely understand what we said. They just don't like it! And when they take the time to once again explain or articulate their concern, and then it's met with the same answer, repeated the same way, they feel unheard and disrespected. They likely are growing angrier by the second. We understand because we've all been that customer.

The solution is to look up from the script and listen—and not just wait for your turn to talk. It doesn't mean that everyone gets what they want, but at least they feel as if they were heard by a real human being, who gave them the respect of considering their unique scenario.

Because when you truly under their situation, you still may have to say no, but you now know enough to perhaps point them to other resources. You can have an authentic conversation with your customers. That's something a chatbot can't do.

Bots can't show authentic empathy—but you can. Bots can't come up with creative solutions or alternatives other than the answers they were programmed to deliver, but when you listen to the nuances and subtleties being communicated, you can. You can also respond much more authentically and address concerns far more effectively.

Here's why you do it: It's one word: predictability. Pre-scripted responses offer a measure of predictability and consistency to our interactions. We know what's profitable in our business and what isn't. The things that are profitable, we agree to. The ones that aren't, or take us off task for too long, we say "no" to. It's businesses.

But here's why we hate it: We don't want to talk to a wall. We get frustrated enough when the chatbot doesn't seem to understand what we're asking for, but when we get the same response from a human being, it brings out the worst in us! Robotic repetition of pre-scripted answers tells us that you aren't listening—and even if you are listening, that you don't care.

Here's a better approach: Don't mimic the worst traits of A.I. Be human and allow those you supervise to be human as well. We certainly have guidelines and policies that we need to stick to, but be authentic enough to engage in meaningful dialogue with your customers and clients.

Truly listen and let them know that they've been heard. Repeat questions back to make sure you understand what they're asking. Look people in the eye when face-to-face, and don't just wait for your turn to talk.

Even if this sounds basic, it isn't anymore. People are being subjected to preprogrammed responses from voice-activated phone menus all the time. You hear it when you call a company and reach a voice menu. You hear a voice at self-checkout informing you that an "unexpected item is in the bagging area." *"How can I help you?"* the chatbot asked with a friendly name and cartoon icon.

Real people are being extracted from the experience and we don't want to see the last remaining vestiges of human interaction relegated to robotic response. Nothing about that feels good.

A.I. may be all the rage, but rage is one thing you certainly don't want your real people creating. Just sayin'.

CHAPTER 22

YOUR CUSTOMERS ARE TELLING YOU MORE THAN YOU REALIZE

We generally have a pretty good read on our customers. We know what they need, and we work hard to deliver it the way they want. That's really the core of business isn't it? But how closely are we really listening? In fact, they're telling us far more than we recognize, and I'll show you how to tune in to this not-so-obvious frequency.

So, I had a layover at Chicago's O'Hare and decided to grab lunch at one of the airport restaurants. My seat was along the railing by the hostess station, facing out to the concourse. Good for people watching. As I sat there, I witnessed a traveler approach the hostess station, ask her a question, and then leave in frustration as she shook her head "no." Then, another traveler asked her the exact same question. Again, the answer was "no," and the potential customer left. Person after person, again and again. The hostess would shake her head and the traveler would leave in frustration. Traveler after traveler. Lost customer. Lost customer. Lost customer.

So, what was the question being asked? In fact, you will not be surprised to learn that this is the most common question asked at airport restaurants:

"Do you have any tables near an electrical outlet?"

Travelers need to be able to recharge their cell phones, laptop computers, and other electrical devises.

This popular restaurant probably lost $500 worth of business in just the 45 minutes that I was there as potential customers walked away. How many customers were they losing every day? That lost revenue could have easily paid for an electrician adding a dozen outlets around the restaurant.

So, how could this restaurant be so clueless as to what so many of their customers were asking for?

> "*Everyone on your team has to understand that their job isn't just doing their job, but helping to grow the business.*"

Here's a more basic question: Do you think those requests were being passed along to her manager? No! It's not her job. Her job is to navigate a busy restaurant with a steady stream of time-crunched travelers and get them a table. To be fair, while she was great at her job, she didn't have a "business growth" mindset. She was focused on her tasks, not on helping to build the business.

Do you have a process in place to document the requests or concerns expressed by your customers or prospects? Do you know when your people are saying "no" to your customers, so you can have the opportunity to consider any changes, accommodations, or enhancements that you might make?

Along those lines, are your people documenting when a customer communicates their frustration? If there were some part of their journey, perhaps a long wait time, a challenge in navigating your app or website, or confusing voice menu, or anything else that they comment or complain to you about, are their superiors made aware of those customers' comments and concerns?

That's the difference between a transactional business and a relational one. Everyone on your team has to understand that their job isn't just doing their job. It's also about helping to grow the business. Every employee has to have, at the foundation of their job description, a mindset that we were hired to help this business be successful. Of course, we have role to play and job to do, but everything we do ultimately has to contribute to our company's success.

So, everything that you see, hear, and come to know over the course of your day, that might impact the business, either positively or negatively, needs to be communicated to those who can affect change. That is also your job.

We've heard the question for years: *"If you see a piece of trash on the floor at your place of work, whose job is it to pick that up?"* We all know by now that it is everyone's job. It impacts how people perceive our business, so it is everyone's job to address it if they encounter it.

The same hold true with customer comments, concerns, and complaints. Even if it's nothing more than something muttered under their breath but is audible to you, then a concern is being articulated. If those in charge don't know about it, how can they be expected to address it? And if it is a problem for one customer, chances are very good that there are many others who feel the same way.

Admittedly, there are some organizations that have learned to tune out comments and complaints. The TSA (our airport screeners in America) have become numb to the countless travelers complaining about the long, slowly moving lines. The audible sighs or comments of *"unbelievable!"* fall largely on deaf ears.

Clerks at the post office are generally efficient, but also seem to have little empathy for those having to wait. That's the hallmark of government workers. Good people to be sure, but they aren't working for businesses in competition with others and don't need to make a profit.

They aren't being evaluated based on the happiness of their "customers," so they appear to not care.

But for those us working in competitive marketplaces, we have to have our radar set to "high." We have to know what our customers, and prospective customers are asking for, or complaining about. And if it turns out to be a common question, comment, or complaint, then we have to address it. But how can we know what our customers are asking for or complaining about if those scenarios aren't passed along to leaders who can affect needed change?

I often hear company leaders boast: *"What sets us apart from our competitors is that we really listen to our customers, and we tailor our solution to their individual needs."* But do you? Really? Come on! Your salespeople might alter their approach based on the customer's unique scenario, but that's different.

Your customers are telling you things—things that are reflective of what they like and don't like about you—but if you're not there to hear it, how do you know it ever even happened? Most often, you don't.

Your job isn't just to do your job. It's also to notice, listen, and share what you've learned so that you can get better.

Here's why you do it: Or maybe why we *don't* do it. I think we don't ask for this kind of internal documentation because we believe we already have a good handle on customers' wants and needs. And to be honest, our employees will always be resistant if they think some new duty is being added to their plate.

"I'm buried as it is," they think out loud. *"Now I'm supposed to do this??"*

But here's why we hate it: We are losing customers. Problems are perpetuating and we can't address something that we don't know about. We know a great deal about our customers to be sure, but if there isn't an expectation of questions and concerns being documented and passed along... well, let's just say that ignorance isn't bliss. It's lost customers and lost revenue. Or worse still, it results in negative online reviews.

Here's a better approach: There should be an expectation and an actual process in place to document and track requests, concerns, or complaints. Someone needs to be responsible for reviewing those reports, and leaders have to take action based on the nature and frequency of those observations.

Like that age-old question: *If a tree falls in the woods and no one is around to hear it, does it make a sound?* Well, if your customers ask for something that you can't accommodate, and no one knows about it, how will you hold on to those whom you disappoint? I think you already know the answer to that.

CHAPTER 23

ANALOGUE THINKING IN A DIGITAL WORLD

Do you ever find yourself marveling (and by marveling, I mean complaining) at how young people often seem to want to skip to the end? They want the reward, but without doing the work. My brilliant colleague and emerging-workforce expert, Eric Chester, helped me understand that young people are just looking at the world through a different lens. Let's discuss how to improve your business by looking at the world through your younger customers' very important eyes.

When I was in college in the early 1980s, we had several full-sized video arcade games in the lobby of my dorm. I had spent a lot of time in middle school and high school at the mall arcade playing games like Pac Man, Asteroids, Dig Dug and Centipede, but there were two machines that I obsessed over in college: Donkey Kong (the original Mario game) and Robotron. I was obsessed. I wasted so much money on those stupid arcade games—25 cents at a time.

In reality, it was a lot of fun and I got pretty good. The goal was to get a little farther in the games each time. Achieving the next level was a small victory and unlocked new challenges, graphics, and bonuses. Of course, you had to start from the beginning each time and each level was a little harder than the last. If you didn't keep up with it, you lost your skills. I can't imagine what my dad would have said if he knew how much money I had spent on those full-sized arcade games trying to beat each level.

I grew up in an analog world. A came before B and you had to get past C, before you could move on to D.

Today's young people are growing up in a very different world. First, they play their video games at home and there is often no cost after you purchased the gaming system. You can play as many times as you want, and you can "die" over and over again with no consequence.

> "If a process seems complicated or overly cumbersome, they will challenge you on it and look for a way to skip past it."

But the biggest change actually came 20 years ago, when "cheat codes" started appearing in online chat rooms. Gamers would find flaws in the system that would allow them to skip levels or beat opponents. These cheat codes were shared and some even appeared in video game magazines. Just like cheating on a test at school, you didn't have to earn your way to passing; you could just cheat your way to the next level.

Today, kids don't have to cheat to skip ahead. They just select the advanced level they want to start on. The gaming companies allow players to choose the level or locations they want to play.

Kids today don't have to listen to an entire album or wait through an 8-track tape to get to their favorite song. They just buy that one song or stream the song they want. The idea of buying an entire album to get the one song that they really want seems ridiculous for them!

By the same token, today's young workers don't want to work for five years to get recognition or a promotion, or 30 years to get the gold watch.

They just go after what they want—now. Waiting is stupid. Waiting is old-fashioned. Waiting is inefficient. Waiting is what old people do.

Eric Chester explained that young people aren't lazy, they just think digitally. There's no reason to go through a meaningless process because that's how it's always been done. Millennials look for ways to circumvent the process, because it makes sense to try to get to the prize in a more creative and expeditious way. They're not being lazy, they're being clever. They are figuring out a better way.

It's the same way they approach ordering, buying, customizing, or contracting. If a process seems complicated or overly cumbersome, they will challenge you on it and look for a way to skip past it.

Of course, we often see the visible signs of their impatience as they throw their hands in the air uttering *"Unbelievable,"* or *"C'mon, really? Give me a break!"* If you listen differently, what they're really saying is: *"This doesn't make sense."*

If your buying process, delivery system, or customer journey doesn't make sense, they will let you know. Actually, we all will. If your process was designed two decades ago, in an analog world, it is time to revisit it.

In an analog world, you balance your checkbook with a pen, stand in line at the bank, fill out a deposit slip, hand it to the teller with a stack of endorsed checks, and then wait as they process them. You might even get to choose a flavored lollipop from the basket for you and your kids when you're done!

In a digital world, you open the bank app on your mobile phone, take a picture of the check, and it's deposited into your account immediately. Actually, that's even antiquated for young people as they all just Venmo money to each other instantaneously.

If things take too much time or require unnecessary work, they'll challenge it—as both employees and as customers. We may characterize them as being lazy, but they think it's ridiculous to waste time and energy on things that don't make sense.

I have struggled with my 17-year-old son over high school algebra.

He constantly questions why he has to spend so much time and so much frustration over something he will never, ever, ever use in his life. Honestly, I don't have a good answer for him other than he's learning to do things he doesn't want to do. That his life will be filled with things that he has to do but doesn't want to. In his mind, that is ridiculous.

When it comes to choosing who to do business with, remember that none of us have to buy from people or companies that we don't like. We don't have to suffer through maddeningly complicated voicemail menus or contact forms, or look up "honey crisp apples" in a grocery store self-checkout menu screen among 23 different varieties of apples, when we know a trained checker could have done it for us in three seconds. We don't have to! We can choose another vendor who doesn't make us do the things we don't want to do.

By and large, young people aren't lazy—they're efficient. They're creative. Sure, they're also impatient and demanding, but so are we. The reality is that they've grown up, and we've grown into, a world that is no longer analog. It's digital.

> **Here's why you do it:** We tend to get frustrated with our younger customers or employees because they seem overly impatient, entitled, and averse to doing the hard work to get things done. In some cases that may be true. But if you look deeper, that aversion to work is often really just a rejection of what they perceive to be meaningless work or processes that don't make sense.
>
> **But here's why we hate it:** We get frustrated at people who get frustrated at us. When someone challenges the way we do things, we think they are a complainer, or being overly demanding. We think: *"Oh, I'm sorry that you don't want to follow the process just like everyone else. Yes, you are special, and we need to do it your way."*
>
> **Here's a better approach:** Try to see your business through a digital lens. Does A really have to come before B and so on? Is there a

way for customer to get to who they want, or what they want without wasting time going through an entire voicemail menu?

In the pitch letters or responses my team sends to keynote speaking prospects, we include a lot of information about my topic, background, and approach, but near the beginning of the pitch letter it says: *"If you want to skip all the information below, just click this link to watch David Avrin's preview video. You'll see in a few short minutes why he is one of the most popular customer-experience speakers in the world today!"*

It's an easy out and quick way to skip ahead. It's a digital link in an analog letter.

Give your customers, both young and old, a way to save time by skipping to what they want or need. Then, not only will they win faster, but you will too.

CHAPTER 24

CROSSING THE CONVERSATION LINE

It's been said for generations that business is about relationships. We do business with people we know, like, and connect with. But when do our conversations with our connections cross a line? How personal is too personal and how can we be our authentic selves without jeopardizing our business relationships? Let's swim through those murky waters together.

People who see me speak at business conferences have admitted to wondering if I'm the same irreverent, confident guy off stage, or if that's just my on-stage persona. I hope they're not disappointed to learn that this is me most all the time. Of course, off duty I'm most often wearing jeans, or shorts, and a super-hero T-shirt. But I made the decision a long time ago to be consistent and authentic both onstage and off. This is me. But it's not all of me. Does that make sense? Everything you see and hear coming out of my mouth on stage and in my video content is all me and what I honestly believe. That said, I don't share everything that I think and feel and believe.

I have opinions about a variety of issues just like everyone else does. I have political and religious beliefs and sports teams that I follow. There are celebrities I can't stand and fashion I think is ridiculous, but I don't share all of that publicly.

Why? Because I have a family to support and employees who rely on me for income. Some people would undoubtedly disagree with my opinions, and that's okay, but why bring those conversations into professional relationships that have nothing to do with my personal preferences?

I've seen too many instances with clients' staff where customer relationships begin to morph into personal friendships. And while deepening relationships are certainly fulfilling—especially when it's someone that you find yourself really liking on a personal level (I'm not talking about romantic feelings; that's a whole different conversation)—I'm referring to real friendships with great people. I'm suggesting that we can't lose sight of the fact that the business dynamics that the relationship is based on, have to take precedence over any perceived personal connection.

"I'm not suggesting that we can't forge meaningful relationships with co-workers, customers, and clients, but we have to be conscious of the lines we shouldn't cross in our conversations."

Remember, this is first and foremost a relationship forged on commerce and we can't confuse it with a personal friendship. That's important because any falling out or disagreement we might have with the individual might adversely affect the revenue of our company. People have lost client contracts over personal issues, and as an employee, you are on the clock. This relationship began with the goal of a financial transaction. Don't let it go off course!

To be clear, I'm not suggesting that we can't forge meaningful relationships with co-workers, customers, and clients, but we have to be conscious of the lines we shouldn't cross in our conversations.

When we start getting a little too comfortable and make comments about a public figure or make an assumption about the political leanings of our client based on earlier comments, we run the risk that they will believe and feel otherwise. Now we've just inserted tension into a relationship that was entirely unnecessary. And none of this has anything to do with our business!

When we get overly comfortable and admit to a crush on a celebrity, or comment on the appearance of someone walking by, or worse yet a coworker, we have crossed a big line! Of course, having thoughts or opinions is perfectly normal. It's human, but we're not at a barbecue with our neighbors, or watching a ball game with our friends! Business is different. It has to be different, and the lines between appropriate and inappropriate conversations are far less grey than they used to be.

To be honest, I struggle with this every day. Not about being inappropriate per se, but about becoming too comfortable and casual with business connections. I often have phenomenal conversations with my clients who are often really brilliant and wonderful people.

When I get off stage after presentation, people are so nice to me! They complement me and smile at me and often want to tell me their stories after hearing my stories on stage. Everyone wants to talk to me like I'm their best friend.

One of things that makes me successful, or so I like to believe, is that I'm personally relatable. I love people and I love talking to people. I am a true extrovert. It's one of the best things about my job. Sure, travel can be exhausting, but I meet so many really wonderful people from around the world. But I also always have to have this active conversation in my head that balances both content and context.

The content is what I'm discussing with someone. The context is the venue and my surroundings and who else is within earshot. It's the reminder that I don't really know this person and I can't talk to them like I would to my wife or my brothers or my best friends. This is hard for me, because I really love to talk to people.

The fact is that I do this for a living. This is my livelihood. My clients are my clients, and the audience members may be friendly, but they aren't my friends. Just one misinterpreted comment or action from the hundreds I may engage with at an event could come back to bite me.

Once again, authentic engagement and comfortable conversation is at the foundation of every beneficial business relationship, but watch the line. There are subjects that families avoid at Thanksgiving and there are subjects and opinions that we should avoid discussing at work with clients and coworkers.

Here's why you do it: What's better than making friends? There are so many things we *have* to do in this life. We need balance. The balance is the things we *get* to do. When we connect with someone who is like us is so many ways, we forge friendships. But when that friendship also involves the exchange of money for goods and services, we have to draw some parameters.

But here's why we hate it: Who wants to put artificial limits on a personal connection? We know them. They're awesome! They're just like us. Right? Well, maybe—and maybe not. Any disagreement, conflict, misinterpreted comment, offensive remark, or overly personal revelation, has the potential to interfere with the exchange of dollars between you. This is business relationship and people's livelihoods are dependent on ongoing business transactions with you.

Here's a better approach: Be professional. Remember that being on-the-clock or on-duty means that you're being paid to interact with your coworkers and clients.

To be fair, we spend a third of our life at work and we should be a great coworker and make wonderful connections with customers and clients. But there is a danger in misinterpreting a smile or a laugh or a conversation. This isn't high school. There are plenty of people to be friends with where you can let you guard down... *after work and on the weekends.* There's just too much at stake to risk your reputation and your job by being too much... *you.*

Be authentic. Be engaging and friendly but remember, this is also your business and your livelihood. Be professional.

CHAPTER 25

CREATING AN ARMY OF AMBASSADORS

It's no mystery that people give more credence to what others say about you than what you say about yourself. So, how do you influence what others say about you? How can we ensure that our customers' positive experiences get shared online and elsewhere? Let's discuss some strategies.

There are few things in life that feel better than praise. As children, we hungered for affirmation from our parents. That pat on the back from our boss fuels our day, and heck, we even shower our pets with praise. *"Good girl! Who's my good girl?"*

Not long ago I was the keynote speaker for a huge dental conference, and following my presentation, I signed copies of my latest book for a line of attendees in the foyer. As people approached the table, they would say wonderfully kind things like:

"Literally, you are the best speaker we've ever had!"

I would smile humbly and respond:

"Thank you so much. That is very kind of you, but keep in mind that your speakers are dentists! I mean, the bar is set pretty low." And we would share a laugh. (To be clear, I love dentists, but their skills are generally limited to being... dentists.)

The truth is, we all have fans for what we do. People appreciate attorneys who defend the innocent, architects who design engaging workspaces, restaurants that offer delicious cuisine, and even movers who take special care of our precious things.

My question for you is this: What happens to all of those positive comments and accolades you receive from your happy customers? What do you do with the words of appreciation and praise you receive for a job well done? Do you simply acknowledge the kind sentiments you receive and thank your customers for thanking you, or do you document them and share them online, or ask them to do it for you?

"*Profitable businesses have happy customers. Successful and growing businesses have vocal fans and have left a trail of happy customers.*"

In other words, do others know how much your fans love you, or are the kind words they offer gone with the wind?

Stop being so modest! There is no shame in getting credit for doing good work. In fact, that's smart business. When choosing a vendor, service provider, or restaurant, we will often seek out others' opinions.

The question is: When people research you online, do they see an endless stream of praise? Do they see nothing? Or worse yet, is there a smattering of complaints?

I can't imagine booking a resort hotel without checking the comments and reviews on Tripadvisor first. It doesn't mean that I trust everything said by everyone, but I'll certainly look for trends and specifics. Why? Because I don't want to take a chance if I'm spending money on a vacation. I don't want to be surprised by something that's subpar.

In that same vein, we will all check out comments left about an ophthalmologist before agreeing to Lasik eye surgery, consumer ratings before buying a vehicle, and Rotten Tomatoes reviews before seeing a movie. It may not directly drive our purchase decision, but it certainly has an influence.

Today, social proof carries a phenomenal amount of weight. When a customer, client, patient, member, or constituent says something kind or complimentary about the work you've provided, ask them to share it with others. Better yet, ask them to do it right then and there.

When someone gives you a professional compliment, pull out your phone, hold it out as if you're about to record a video, and ask: *"Would you mind saying that again?"*

I'm serious! Hand-held, authentic comments, taken at the moment that emotions are high and compliments are heartfelt, is incredibly impactful. Sitting in front a webcam two days later with a scripted or rehearsed endorsement carries far less weight.

"I have to tell you" (said awkwardly and overly-rehearsed), *"Dr. Carter was so wonderful to work with. She really seemed to care about my family and me. I finally have the smile I always wanted, and I would highly recommend her to anyone looking for prosthodontist."*

Really? Yuck. In an effort to "to get it right" it ends up looking inauthentic and rehearsed. But endorsements offered when emotions are running high are real and credible and influential.

"I've got to tell you... Oh my God! If I had any idea how great my smile would look. I'm sorry." (Sniff, sniff.)

"I'm just really happy. Look! Amazing! Why did I wait? Why did I wait?? Thank you! Thank you! I'm telling you that Doctor Carter is a miracle worker. I love her! What she's done for me. I'm sorry. I'm just feeling emotional."

Right? So, which one is more credible? Which approach is more believable and influential?

Of course, not every experience elicits tears and over-the-top emotion, but regardless of your industry, you have happy customers or clients. They have their way of expressing their gratitude and it likely mirrors what others feel about you as well.

All too often we're reluctant to ask because we don't want to bother someone with a request for a video or writing a simple letter. Some feel as if it's imposing on their customers. Others feel as if it's unprofessional. The truth is that we are all in business and our customers certainly understand this. They're the ones spending money with us for crying out loud! They get it. More importantly, they like us. Who better to ask for some kind words?

This isn't about over-surveying everyone who might have come into contact with you and your business. That is an imposition. I'm talking about a little special request from the people who love you! They're the ones most likely to say "yes" and the ones whose feedback is the most beneficial to your business.

Most often, all it takes is a tilting of your head slightly to the side and placing your hand on your chest to show your appreciate and measure of humility, and then saying humbly:

"Thank you so much for the kind words. I can't tell you how much we appreciate your feedback. Honestly, this is what fills our tank each day and why we do what we do. So, may I ask for a quick favor?"

Profitable businesses have happy customers. Successful and growing businesses have vocal fans and have left a trail of happy customers. Friends, the world is different today and many, if not most of your prospects, will look you up before doing business with you. Make sure they get an accurate view of how they will feel after they give you their business.

Here's why you do it: We're often reluctant to ask people to say nice things about us because we think it makes us look needy or insecure. *"Praise me. Like me. Tell me how pretty I am!"* But business isn't like that. It's business.

But here's why we hate it: What we hate is being let down. As customers, we hate feeling like we got fooled or taken advantage of, or that we just didn't matter to a company we chose to do business with. The best way to hedge our bets is to find out what others thought about you before we give you our money. If we don't see a critical mass of positive comments, we see you as a risk. That risk drives us to your competitors

Here's a better approach: Share the praise you receive with the world—or at least your market. It's not boastful. It's business! It's not bragging. It's proof of good work. Being the best-kept secret is not something to be proud of. It's a company to avoid.

Listen, advertising goes back to the dawn of civilization. Telling the world: *"I'm really great!"* is just a form of advertising. Those words coming *from* you are taken with a grain of salt. But when everyone else says that you're great, well, that's social proof.

CHAPTER 26

THE SERENDIPITY FACTOR

One of the lasting legacies of the global pandemic is the rapid rise and growing comfort level with virtual connections. Generations of science fiction stories feature the recurring theme of a world in which people never actually meet each other. Covid-19 has in many ways, accelerated what has long been predicted. Of course, face-to-face connections will never be completely eliminated. There is too much value generated from unexpected encounters. Let's talk about the importance of getting our feet back under the same table.

About 10 years ago, I flew to Philadelphia from my home in Denver, Colorado, to spend a day helping a very successful friend and colleague refine her message and her marketing strategy. She kindly offered to pick me up at the Philadelphia airport, and after gathering my luggage, I met her curbside. She drove up, gave her a smile and wave and I loaded my suitcase in the back of her car. As I climbed into the passenger side, she paused, looked me up, and down and said quite bluntly:

"Don't ever get off an airplane looking like that again."

I laughed and said: *"What? We're friends. It's not like you're seeing me for the first time. This is my favorite superhero T-shirt."*

"You're not understanding me," she continued. *"A T-shirt and shorts may be comfortable for you, but you have no idea who you didn't meet today. You*

have no idea what consulting gig you didn't get because of the way you look. Professionals didn't engage with you on that flight and nobody was curious about your business because they didn't know that you have a business—because you don't look like a professional today."

I didn't have a response. She was absolutely right. I took a day off to travel and my business essentially closed for the duration of that trip.

Her point wasn't about "dressing for success" as much as acknowledging the importance of serendipity: chance encounters that create beneficial business opportunities.

"What's lost in the physical separation, is the possibility of happenstance — the ideas that come from chance encounters and unplanned discussions."

Ideas come from conversation, and information is transferred in conversation. But conversations don't happen without connection. While we can certainly communicate remotely, real connection is enhanced by proximity and a dynamic that allows for it, encourages it, and acknowledges it.

Much of the shift we have seen in recent years is a shift away from in-person connection. In the interest of simplifying our business models, streamlining an ordering process, facilitating a transaction, expediting the delivery, lowering our costs, and even steering clear of disease, we have too often extracted humans from our business process. In doing so, we have also eliminated in large part, the "Serendipity Factor."

How often is our most valuable feedback and the most creative ideas a direct result of direct interaction with our customers and clients? What business insights have come from coworkers during chance encounters in the breakroom, or people stopping by our desk to run something by us, or conversations in the hallways between sessions during a conference or convention?

While the coronavirus taught many of us that we can work from home, businesses realized long ago the advantages of allowing employees to work from home. It's not really new, just more pervasive. But there are some distinct disadvantages as well. Sure, we can collaborate via video chat, but those conversations are almost always scheduled, right?

What's lost in the physical separation is the possibility of happenstance—the ideas that come from chance encounters and unplanned discussions. It's the bouncing off of each other, the field-testing of ideas, or the playing devil's advocate that can keep us from wasting time on things where we otherwise lacked perspective.

Put more succinctly, accidental encounters can often produce profound epiphanies.

Dating websites and apps are a great, structured way to "virtually" meet someone who is also looking to meet someone. But how many great relationship and wonderful marriages were the result of catching someone eye at the grocery store, a chance encounter at the park, or a business introduction that grew into a personal connection? Should we just dismiss the potential benefit of people meeting by chance?

To be clear, the idea of serendipity doesn't suggest leaving creativity to blind luck. I'm suggesting making space for unexpected connection. Serendipity in business is where proximity meets creativity. The result is often opportunity.

The point is that when you allow for your people to meet with your customers more often, you create scenarios for beneficial and informative interactions, communication, and conversation with each other. And in that interaction, you increase the chances that you'll learn something valuable.

When you force your important clients to communicate with you over email, on a contact form, or with a chatbot, you may have saved yourself time, but you've also robbed your business of an interaction that might provide insight, opinion, and the nuance that comes from human conversation.

Automated online chat and voice menus don't care how frustrated a customer might be, but you should. Autoresponders have no stake in whether a delivery is postponed, but your business lives or dies on how satisfied your customer are.

When it comes to fleshing out ideas, it's hard to simply trust your own judgment, but when you invite bright, insightful others into the conversation, 2 + 2 equal 10... or 20, or 30.

The business landscape is littered with success stories that started with a chance encounter. Some of the biggest business problems were uncovered by a customer or client and passed along during a face-to-face conversation with a staff member. Conferences, conventions, staff meetings and retreats are important examples of scheduled proximity that can lead to unexpected conversations and unique solutions.

Most clients or customers leave you for reasons you will never know. But meaningful conversations between your real team members and customers can result in the sharing of important information that can help you hold onto them.

Effective virtual interactions between your business and your customers will become an increasingly important element in your business model, but don't eliminate the opportunity for in-person connection or collaboration as well. What you'll miss will be more valuable than what you save.

> **Here's why you do it:** We often look to reduce the human element because humans are expensive, unpredictable, inconsistent, and not always reliable. Working virtually makes sense, and many have been asking for more flexibility. Reducing costs while increasing predictability is something we can actually control and budget for. It's smart business.

> **But here's why we hate it:** As employees, we may love the flexibility of working remotely, but we also lose out on more meaningful

connection with coworkers and the energy that comes from proximity. We miss the creativity bolstered by collaboration. It can get lonely.

As customers, we get frustrated having to spend time learning your voicemail system when we often just need to talk to a real person. Personal connection with your customers just gets things done faster.

Here's a better approach: While you look to create efficiencies for your business and your customers, also look for ways to increase face time between you and your customers as well. Foster physical proximity between your staff and their colleagues.

The best ideas are often enhanced though the back and forth of creation borne of conversation. The most glaring deficiencies in your business model are often brought to light by what is being shared with you by your customers and clients. We have to create the venues and opportunities for those conversations to occur.

Some of the most valuable information is shared person to person. Those conversations can be spontaneous, or even through the scheduled serendipity of a weekly organizational Morning Huddle! (www.CustomerExperienceAdvantage.com)

It's been said that when you talk, you only know what you know. But when you connect and listen to others, you not only know what you know, but now you know what they know, and that knowledge gives you power.

In recent years, I've earned multiple six figures from business relationships that resulted from chance encounters while traveling. And not one of them occurred while I was wearing a T-shirt and shorts. Just sayin'.

CHAPTER 27

THE POWER OF PLAYING SECOND FIDDLE

We live in a world that celebrates entrepreneurship and leading in business. We've been conditioned to believe that true success comes from inventing something or being in charge. But reality reflects something very different for the vast majority of us. I want to offer a new perspective on the crucial role that most people play in business success.

My brother-in-law is an amazing fiddle player. In fact, Matt Schumacher is one of the best fiddle players on the planet. Call it a violin if you want, but Matt plays country music and he's done so with some the biggest names in country music even though you've likely never heard his name before.

Matt played in international youth orchestras at age seven and alongside the best adults in the world by fourteen. He earned scholarships and awards and eventually made the shift from playing classical music to country. Today, in his early forties, there are few on the planet that can play at his level. He's a true savant and a really great guy!

As mesmerizing as it is to watch him play, what really strikes me is how he describes the part he really plays. Despite his freakish talent, he's very clear that his role is not to be the leader. This isn't about humility.

"My job," says Matt, *"is to help make everyone around me...better."* And every musician around him plays at the top of their game while having a great time in the process. It's truly awesome to witness.

Think about the things that you do that you seem to do better because of the skills of those around you.

> "Just as a chain is only as strong as its weakest link, so too can a team be stronger because of its strongest members."

When I play tennis against someone better than me, I just play better. When you are in a brainstorming session with really smart people, doesn't everyone seem to contribute better ideas? That's the essence of the mastermind model, right? Smart leaders surround themselves with high performers who collectively raise each other's level of performance.

So, here's my question: Do you make others around you better?

It's certainly not in your job description to raise others' performance. You're expected to do your job well and serve your customers with excellence. But doesn't excellence also inspire excellence?

There's a great line in the movie: *As Good as it Gets* when Jack Nicholson's character says to Helen Hunt's: *"You make me want to be a better man."*

It is such a profound moment in a great movie. It's a line that's been recounted often by others who recognize the power of being around someone who demonstrates excellence, empathy, forgiveness, or any of the qualities that we might admire. They make us want to be *that* good. They give us something to aspire to.

Now to be clear, I'm not referring to hyper-competitive sales cultures where the leaderboard is posted for all to see, with overt competition and jockeying for dominance and rewards for performance. But to be clear, I'm not criticizing that either. It's a proven sales culture model that can produce strong results and people generally know what they're signing up for.

What I'm talking about is a personal commitment to deliver excellence, high-level performance, service delivery, and *your* contribution to your team or organization's success.

Just as a chain is only as strong as its weakest link, so too can a team be stronger because of its strongest members.

Organizations that set a high bar in terms of their collective performance and behavioral expectations are proven to have higher employee and customer satisfaction. Excellence begets excellence and excellence feels better than average—for both your team and your customers!

When that higher level of service, attentiveness, accommodation, and effort is observed by others on the team, a new sense of what's possible or even expected is created. The "A" players create a "new normal" that others rise to. Those that don't, become evident very quickly.

This new level of service can become a catalyst for conformity in your company. In other words, there can be a new internal standard driven by someone on the team who made everyone around them better—simply by being better.

Some of the best behavior—let me rephrase that—*most* of the best behavior in terms of service excellence doesn't come from management. It comes from great team members who take it upon themselves to step up and maximize their supporting role. In doing so, they show others around them what's possible.

The truth is that everyone in your organization is in charge. You're in charge of your attitude and behavior. You're in charge of your learning and meeting your deadlines. You're in charge of your preparation, contribution, and how you serve your customers.

Konstantin Stanislavski famously said, *"There are no small parts, only small actors."* In those well-crafted words, he was reminding all his players that the importance on stage is not reserved for the lead actors.

In business, we are all on stage. Everyone is watching—and not just from outside your business—but internally well. The question is: When you perform, what do others see?

Here's why you do it: It's easy to lose sight of the bigger picture when we have so much to do. We think, *"I have enough to do with my own job. How am I supposed to be responsible for how others perform? Seriously? How about I do me and you do you?"*

But here's why we hate it: Your brand, in the mind of your customers, is often based on the last encounter they had with you regardless of who on your team it was with. To your customers, you are all on the same level. They don't want to have to escalate a matter to leadership. They want everyone to step up and deliver with excellence.

Here's a better approach: Help your organization and everyone on the team to be more successful by raising your own game. It may not be in your job description to "make everyone around you better," but it can be your personal commitment to perform at a higher level. In doing so, you will make others better. Your customers will notice and give you more of their business.

"A" players don't have to be the highest-ranking members of the organizations. "A" players are simply the most effective ones.

Listen, 99% of us will never be the boss, but being a member of the team doesn't mean that you have less impact. To the contrary, you can have more!

The *Cambridge Dictionary* defines the term "second fiddle" as "to be less important or in a weaker position than someone else."

I guarantee you that Matt Schumacher, in his powerful supporting role, isn't playing second fiddle to anyone. Just sayin'.

CHAPTER 28

ALL THEY CARE ABOUT IS PRICE

I was talking to a client recently who commented that it almost doesn't matter anymore what they do to market their business. The only thing that customers care about is price. Oh, that is so not true! It only appears to be true. Let's explore your crucial role in dispelling this myth.

Have you ever gotten an email, in which everything in the message is in all capital letters and every word is in bold? THE ENTIRE MESSAGE IS IN ALL CAPS! It's sort of the digital text version of shouting a message to someone.

More likely, what the author is saying is: *"This is really important! Pay attention to this message."* (Or, *"I'm really mad at you right now!"*)

The problem is that when everything is in bold, it's hard to decipher which part of the message is really important. I mean, is every part of the letter or message meant to be shouted, or just the specific angry parts?

The point is that when everything is bold, then functionally nothing is in bold. Nothing stands out. It all has equal weight. It's all the same.

That's what tends to happen with marketing approaches as well. When we all promote the same pedestrian claims of quality, integrity, trust, commitment, etc., or we boast about how "our people make the difference," the marketplace goes numb. In essence, we're all saying that we're all really good and that we all really care. Yawn.

All They Care About is Price

It's virtually impossible to tell the differences between most auto parts stores, or personal injury law firms, credit card companies, cell phone carries, burger joints, and more. And if you are in the B2B space, it's even more difficult, as all of the options available are certainly qualified at a minimum.

The manufacturing companies can all make that sure that their quality parts fit. The accounting software programs all manage your finances effectively, and the supply chain consultants, one would assume, understand the ins and outs of supply chain management.

> "The four most dangerous words to your business are: 'All Things Being Equal.' When we believe you are just like your competitors, then of course it's about price!"

The point is that we, as consumers, assume that every legitimate business option today is qualified to do the work. In fact, they have to be, or they wouldn't survive. They have to be, or they would be "outed" on social media or online review sites. Today, everyone is good—or at least good enough.

You've heard the question: "What do you call the person who graduated dead last in their medical school graduating class?" Answer: Doctor! They all passed the test. It doesn't mean that they graduated at the top of their class, but we assume they all know what they're doing—and they certainly know more than we do!

One of your biggest barriers to sales and growth is the fact that your potential customers believe that there isn't a significant difference between you and the other players in your space. The fact that *you* know the difference doesn't mean a whole lot. *They* have to.

I was consulting with a successful prosthodontist dental practice outside of New York City. They were lamenting that prospective patients were calling and inquiring about expensive dental implants, but they only cared about the price. I disagreed.

"*No, you don't understand,*" they insisted. "*We get calls all day long and they tell us that they just want a price quote. They don't want to have to come in. They just want the price. That's all they care about.*"

I insisted again that it was simply not true.

The problem that these professionals were facing, and that many of us in business face, is the assumption of quality. When your prospects assume that all of your legitimate competitors can provide the same quality options that you can, then they just search for the best price. Who wouldn't?

To be clear, this dental practice's prospective patients had already done research online (like we all do) and had already weeded out the unqualified players. And because the marketing claims were largely the same from those final dental practices under consideration, they assumed that the only meaningful difference was the price. Those prospective dental patients actually cared a great deal about the qualifications and experience of the dentists. They cared about the quality of the dental work, but by the time they called their office, it had come down to price. The calls the dental office had been receiving were at the end of the process. They just didn't realize it had been going on largely without them.

I've been saying this for a decade: The four most dangerous words to your business are: "all things being equal." When we believe you're just like your competitors, then of course it's about price!

Now, to be clear, I've heard authors, speakers, and others who say things like, "*If you just do blank and blank in your business, then price is no longer an issue.*" That's garbage. Price is always an issue. I'm not naive. But as long as you're priced competitively, and others charge in the same ballpark, then price isn't the issue. They can afford you or they can't. The same holds true for your competitors.

Your challenge is commoditization.

Friends, we can never, ever, ever allow ourselves to become equal in the minds of our customers. We bring different skillsets, talent, staff, experience, buying process, products, perspective, location, or hours. But if they think we're the same, then it will be about price—or proximity. Whoever is the cheapest and closest wins! Do you really aspire to be the "low-price leader" in your category? Yuck.

Here's the uncomfortable truth. If your customers or prospects believe that you are essentially the same as your competitors, that's your fault. But it's also your opportunity to envision, create, and communicate true differentiation. It is your opportunity to enhance you customers' experience in ways that spur them to become raving fans who sing your praises to others.

Look at your job function within your organization. If you are doing exactly what you're supposed to do, if you as a company are seen as doing exactly what your competitors do, then you are merely competent. What we have to become is preferable. We have to become talked about and shared and endorsed.

Being really, really good at what you do isn't a competitive advantage today. It's just the entry fee. Being good gives you permission to enter the market and play the game. The question most prospects have isn't *"Can you?"* it's *"Why you?"*

Here's why you do it: We tend to promote the same things as our competitors because what we say about ourselves is true. We do offer quality, convenience, passion, and great people. It's also the same claims along the lines of: Our customers come first, quality is job-one, or we only use the freshest ingredients that we hear others use as well. It makes sense.

But here's why we hate it: As consumers, whether B2C or B2B, we've grown numb to most marketing claims. You're good at what you do. We get it. You really care. We get it. How much do you charge?

Here's a better approach: Don't just focus on being good. Work harder to be different. Help customers recognize your unique products, broader customization options, or streamlined process *before* they get to the question of price.

On your easy-to-navigate website, highlight what you do or offer that others don't. Simplify your buying process or bolster your conversations to leave customers feeling that they got more than they expected, and faster than expected. *That* is a customer experience worth talking about—and we want people to talk about us!

Once again, being priced competitively is a foundational tenet of a strong business model, but if you find yourself being hammered on price by your customers, you now know the reason. Don't simply join that painful and unprofitable race to the bottom, but instead focus on communicating and demonstrating what's different.

Friends, don't be shy about shouting your uniqueness from the mountaintop. Just don't use all caps.

CHAPTER 29

KEEP IT TO YOURSELF

It seems these days that whatever you think, say, or post online, there are people just waiting by their keyboard to disagree with you, question your intelligence, your morality, or patriotism. It's hard balancing our right to free expression with trying to run a business that appeals to everyone and not just with those who agree with us. So, how do you achieve that balance? You may not like my answer.

When I was a kid, I remember wondering why we weren't rich. I mean, it's not just that I *wanted* to be rich. I think every kid wants to be rich, but I wondered why we weren't.

I mean, my father was an actual rocket scientist who designed and built instruments and experiments that traveled on rocket ships. Some of those experiments are right now sitting on the surface of other planets! How could we possibly not be rich?

I remember asking him, on more than one occasion: *"Dad, how much money do you make?"*

His answer was always the same: *"It's none of your business."*

He wasn't trying to be mean. He was just teaching me what was, and was not, socially acceptable. When I protested, he would say: *"David, there are just some things you don't talk about in mixed company."* Chief among them were money and politics.

He went on to explain that when you reveal things about yourself that others don't share in common with you, or discuss subjects that people are very opinionated about, it creates a feeling of separation. You are putting a wall between you. He told me that our relationships are based on what we have in common, not on what we don't. So we avoid talking about things that push us apart. Wise words.

Coincidentally, I wrote this Huddle essay on what would have been my father's 84th birthday. I wish he were still here, and that his mindset was more prevalent today.

> "Sure, you have freedom of speech, but you don't have freedom from the consequences of the speech you choose to share."

But we all know that the world has changed. It seems there is nothing we don't talk about or argue about, as we are more polarized than ever.

We used to say things like: *"We can just agree to disagree,"* and *"Everyone has the right to their own opinion."* Today we give everyone *our* opinion. Today, we are right, and the other side is wrong—and not just wrong, they're idiots, evil, and everything that's wrong with the world!

Do you see where this is going?

To be clear, I'm not here to lament the current state of public discourse. I'm here to help you separate your personal opinions from the customers who have the power to separate you from their money.

The point is that you have the right to believe whatever you believe! No matter which side of any issue, I respect your right to read what you want, listen to whichever pundit, or debate whatever ideology supports your worldview.

But don't believe for a second that your business life and private life are completely separate. In the age of social media and cell phone cameras that document our lives, nothing is separate. Sure, you have freedom of speech, but you don't have freedom from the consequences of the speech you choose to share.

There are nearly eight billion people living in the world today, and most of them don't believe what you believe. Think about it. From politics, religion, child-raising, guns, climate change, privacy, social distancing, Kardashians and eating meat, the world is full of different opinions.

There's a great line that says: *"Opinions are like (a specific body part). Everyone has one."* Most of them don't align with yours.

So, in business, why would we intentionally aggravate, alienate, or drive an unnecessary wedge between us and the people we hope will spend money with us? While people hold vastly different beliefs, what we all have in common is the practical value of the money in our pocket.

Money doesn't care what you believe. Money is universal in its ability to purchase food for our families, services for our business, furniture for our homes, and the freedom to enjoy the things in life that we all work hard for.

Your money spends just the same as someone else's. Welcome one and all!

When your publicly expressed (but divisive) opinions drive a wedge between you and your customers, we get a short-lived victory of feeling right, of winning the argument. But we've also likely lost sales revenue that pays our team, feeds our family, and keeps our business viable. If you post divisive comments or rants on social media, or forward politicized memes, you are leaving a virtual paper trail of "customer repellant."

When you get into a prolonged argument with someone online, growing more and more insulting with each post, you are losing with every "obvious" point that you think you're winning. I've seen numerous social media posts that say things like: *"If you agree with this or that, unfriend me now."* Wow. Are people that disposable? Are customers that replaceable?

Statistically, as many as half of all your customers will hold different political views than you do. Of course, if we were all independently wealthy, we could afford to anger half of our prospective customers. I'm not.

To be clear, you have every right to believe what you believe! I'm not suggesting for a minute that you don't have the right to stand your ground and make your case, or even forward an article or a divisive picture. I'm just questioning the wisdom of wearing your opinions on your sleeve.

Please don't dismiss my words as advocating for one side or the other, and don't make assumptions. You don't know what I believe, and that the point.

I have a family to feed, college to pay for, and employees who rely on me. I have opinions and discussions and debates; they're just not for the world to see.

Connecting with our audience and tapping into the commonality of customers is a business magnet. Unnecessary controversy is a customer repellent. What are you spraying around?

Here's why you do it: We offer our opinions on controversial subjects because they are, by their very nature, important. Things are messed up and we have ideas about the best ways to fix them. Or we see something that bothers us, and we feel the need to weigh in. Things matter and sometimes we don't want to sit on the sidelines. Some things just need to be said!

But here's why we hate it: Yuck. It just feels bad. I mean, we don't have to agree about everything, just don't be mean-spirited, or try to shove your position down our throats. Don't forward things that may not be true just because it supports your viewpoint and you saw it on the internet. It's too easy to just not buy from you if you make us feel uncomfortable, or worse yet—disrespected.

Here's a better approach: You may not like this, but here goes. Keep your polarizing opinions to yourself, or within your circle of friends and family and off of social media and out of your conversations with clients or customers. Scrub your social media of past divisive comments or posts, and don't forward insulting memes.

Only a few times, if ever, in modern history has anyone ever been persuaded to change their opinions because they saw a clever picture with an outrageous caption. We're just preaching to others who agree with us anyway. So, what is that solving? How much time are we wasting arguing with TylerG, ImRightUrWrong27, or Babyface JennaGirl? C'mon, really? You're better than that.

People have lost their businesses, investors have lost their money, and people have lost jobs because they spouted-off about something unrelated to their company role or posted pictures of their off-duty partisan activities. There is too much at stake.

Listen, your clients and prospects will look you up online. You do! Do they see someone like them, someone who seems likable or reasonable, or do they see someone on the other side?

Of course, you don't have to be a rocket scientist to recognize that polarizing opinions don't foster great relationships with customers and clients. Engage in conversations that attract people and create connection. I promise, you'll have a better chance to win in business and in life.

And that lesson, not surprisingly, I learned from a rocket scientist. Thanks, Dad.

CHAPTER 30

DON'T POSTURE

A hundred and fifty years ago, before modern medicine, traveling salespeople would sell "snake oil" as a cure-all for a variety of ailments. Of course, by the time people realized that the medicine didn't work, the salesman was long gone. Today, there is nowhere to hide. I want to talk about how business today is viewed in the bright light of day.

About 25 years ago, after a decade as an employee, I left my full-time public relations job to start my own marketing and PR firm. I was on my own for the first time with limited resources and my early clients were mostly small companies and entrepreneurs.

I remember being envious of those who had coworkers, or an actual assistant to help them get things done. I was scratching my way to make a living, working 60-hour weeks finding clients and promoting their companies. I really needed some help, but I couldn't afford it at the time. One of my clients had a phenomenal assistant named Jay Foboda.

The guy was great. Literally, like a dream assistant. He answered the phone, wrote client letters, and managed his calendar. He was *exactly* what I needed.

So, I was having lunch with my client one day and I commented that I wished I had the money to hire someone like Jay. He just smiled, *"Oh, you do,"* he said.

"Yeah, I wish," I replied. *"I hope to be in a position to pay someone in about six months.*

"*I don't pay Jay anything,*" he said with a smile.
"*How is he working for nothing?*" I asked, exasperated.
"*It's me!*" he says with a full belly laugh at this point. "*Jay doesn't exist.*"
"*I've talked to him a dozen times!*" I insist.
"You mean you talked to this eager young man: "*Hey, let's get something on the calendar for next Thursday,*" he says changing his voice.

He made him up! In an effort to make his company look bigger than it was, he actually made up a personal assistant!

Now remember, this was the early 1990s, and with the internet as a new, widespread resource, more entrepreneurs were starting to work at home. But even so, they were concerned they would not be seen as a "real business."

As an aside, if you are under 35 years old, and wonder what the internet was like back then, Search "dial-up modem sound" and imagine each page taking 45 seconds to load. But I digress.

So, to avoid the stigma of the home office, people would put their home address on their business card, but would list their office as "Suite 120." Of course, Suite 130 was the kitchen and 210 was the master bedroom...

Even today, people do all sorts of things to posture, trying to look bigger than they are, or more successful. It's all along the flawed advice to "fake it until you make it." Bad strategy. Today, you can't fake anything.

To be clear, posturing is not the same as positioning. In business, we always want to highlight our best qualities and our most appealing "features and benefits," positioning ourselves as the best choice to our clients and prospects. But posturing is different.

Have you ever noticed on LinkedIn, for example, that hundreds of thousands of individual service providers, or solopreneurs, list themselves as "President and CEO"—of a one-person firm?

When I left my employer and went out on my own in 1995, my company was called The Avrin Public Relations Group. My brother teased me and said: "*No, you're the Avrin Public Relations guy.*"

We were all trying to do the best we could to compete, and appearing bigger meant being more credible or more capable.

Today, we live in a different world. Competition is certainly tougher with all the new players and a world of competitors. What is easier today is our ability to sniff-out inauthentic claims. Falsified résumés or dubiously claimed accomplishments will ultimately be uncovered. You can't fake or overstate anything anymore.

> "I'm not suggesting that you can't be creative in your marketing or sales approach. I'm just saying you can't be creative with the truth."

We've learned that Amazon bestsellers are not necessarily real bestsellers, and "award-winning" companies, products, or professionals, might have that award bought and paid for or bestowed by a questionable source.

The point is that transparency and authenticity is more important today than ever. Virtually anything that you claim can be checked.

During challenging times, we often see companies and professionals expanding beyond their wheelhouse to go after any work that might help pay the bills—even if it's a bit of a stretch in terms of their capabilities. And while I applaud and absolutely encourage my clients to be clear on their core competency and find new customers who might need their skills and capabilities, there is a real danger in saying "yes" to everything. There's a danger in claiming skills or capacities for things you haven't done before and thinking to yourself: *Just get the contract and we'll figure it out.*

There's a danger in exaggerating the recognition you've received, or the results that you'll deliver for your clients, trying anything to win the business over your competitors. Eventually you will have to deliver on that exaggerated promise, or someone else on your team will have to deliver what *you* promised.

Just know that your promised deliverable will see the light of day eventually, and the backlash from a less-than-pleased customer or client might be plastered all over the internet for the world to see. You may have won the short battle to get the business, but you're losing the war.

I know, it seems basic: *Say what you'll do, and do what you say.* And while it's simple, it's not always easy when we are competing with others and sales revenue is on the line. But integrity in business—authenticity in business—is the foundation for building your reputation and fortifying your brand.

Of course, I'm not suggesting that you can't be creative in your marketing or sales approach. I'm just saying you can't be creative with the truth.

When you start talking about "grey areas," you are stepping into dangerous territory. Don't go there.

Great conversations with your customers don't need to include exaggerations. Great service doesn't mean fake smiles, and great experiences don't have to include "wow" moments. Sometimes success comes from just being great and delivering great.

Listen, we're all customers as well, and as customers, we have our radar cranked pretty high these days. We can sniff out bluster.

Don't posture. Don't tell people what we want to hear. Tell them the truth in the most authentic, believable, and persuasive manner possible. If we can trust your words and your approach, we'll be much more likely to trust you with our business.

Here's why you do it: We learned at an early age to put our best foot forward. The words we say made an impact, and if we can say things that make people go, "wow!", even better!

But here's why we hate it: We all remember that kid in the neighborhood who used to make stuff up to impress the other kids. Their grandfather invented ice cube trays, or they had an expensive yacht—except nobody was allowed to ride on it. Yeah, right.

In business, we know those people too. There's always just enough truth to make their claims seems plausible, but we don't really trust them.

Here's a better approach: It's important to recognize that the rules have changed. Ironically, they've changed into what they should have been all along.

Don't exaggerate what you're able to deliver. Don't inflate your capabilities. Don't go after or accept work that you can't complete at a high level. Be honest, enthusiastic, and deliver exactly what you say you can—and then do it better than others in your industry! Authenticity helps build a reputation that can grow your business.

Because today Jay Foboda would be unmasked and out of a job pretty quickly—along with the guy who hired him. Just sayin'.

CHAPTER 31

HAVING A BAD DAY

So, as I write this, I have been suffering from a persistent cough for the past few weeks and it's been really frustrating trying to get through a single sentence without coughing. Regardless, I'm going to load up on meds and power through because I have an obligation to my clients, just as you have an obligation to show up and deliver for your customers and clients. Let's talk about doing what needs to be done when we don't feel like doing anything at all.

We all have bad days. Some people have bad weeks! The challenge is to balance your right to be human with your company's need to deliver for your customers day in and day out. So how do you balance your right to be less than ideal from time to time with the obligation you have to the people who are paying you for that day's work?

Most often, the struggles we deal with are simply minor inconveniences—like a cough—but other times persevering through adversity can border on heroic.

Many of us all remember the 1996 Summer Olympics in Atlanta when Gymnast Kerri Strugg famously sprinted toward the vault and delivered for her team in the final moments of a competition—on a broken ankle! Other athletes have stepped up during important games playing through a bout with the flu, or suffering some other injury or ailment.

And, of course, countless moms and dads take care of their kids while pushing through illnesses of their own. As parents, we don't get to take time off of parenting when our kids need us. It's part of the job description.

But we don't need to be heroic to deal with minor adversity at work. We've all been in situations where a restaurant server was clearly overwhelmed with too many tables because someone had called in sick. Even if the service was less than ideal, we can certainly be compassionate and empathize with a server being pushed to their limit.

> "We all go through stuff, but we also have a contract with our employer and a covenant with our customers to deliver an hour's work for an hour's pay—at a high level!"

Then again, what of those with back stories or hardships that we don't know about? We only see the resulting distraction, disconnection, and maybe even rude behavior they display.

"Sorry, I'm just having a bad day." They say with a loud sigh.

Or what about those who don't say it? They just show it on their face, their actions and behavior. *"Whoa. Someone is pretty nasty today,"* we mutter to ourselves. Often their behavior or inattention doesn't come across in a way that makes us sympathetic, but just makes them look angry, rude, or like they just don't care.

Listen, we can all empathize with tough days, but you never know who might not recognize your struggle and misinterpret your attitude. Then again, there are those who might recognize what you're dealing with, but not really care. I mean, *"Sorry that your dog kept you up all night, but I've been waiting for 20 minutes for someone to help me."*

This is a tough subject because it's a balancing act. Sometimes we just don't care, but we have to just pretend to care. Our job is our job and we're being paid to show up, put on a good face, and deliver for our coworkers, customers, and clients regardless of how we're feeling.

To be clear, this is not about being "fake." But sometimes "faking it" is the most human and giving thing we can do. It can be a real act of service to not burden others with our stuff.

For example, when I get hired to travel to a conference and deliver a keynote presentation or lead a strategic session, it doesn't matter how many travel disruptions I've experienced along the way. It doesn't matter to the meeting planner, the client, and the audience that my luggage didn't make the connection, or I that arrived at 2:00 a.m. and only got three hours of sleep. They made an investment in me. Professionals paid their registration fees and traveled from distant cities to attend the event. They expect to get what they paid for.

Trust me, there's a lot often happens behind the scenes and I have some pretty brutal days—as you do as well. But my audiences and my consulting clients will never, ever, ever know about it!

I'm not heroic. I'm just fully cognizant that my clients don't really care what kind of day I'm having. It's not that they are uncaring. They care a lot. They care about their company and their people and their audience—*as they should!*

My job is to deliver, regardless of my circumstance, and I'm getting paid to show up on time, deliver great content and serve my clients regardless of the day I'm having.

This is a really significant issue because every day we encounter, or engage with, dozens, if not hundreds of people. Odds are good that many, if not most of them, are going through something. Real people have complicated lives and challenging days. But don't we have an obligation to our company and our customers to put on a brave face the best we can?

Of course, any one of us can face profound circumstances that might affect us on a deep or debilitating level. In most of those instances, we're probably not working that day anyway. But most of the crud we go through isn't profound, it's just a hassle.

We get calls from home because our kids are fighting. An egg-salad sandwich may not agree with us, or maybe just some lingering issue or conflict with our spouse or significant other has us upset and less-than-focused. That's life.

We all go through stuff, but we also have a contract with our employer and a covenant with our customers to deliver an hour's work for an hour's pay—at a high level! When we are on, we need to be on.

Please don't misinterpret all of this as being unfeeling or insensitive. To the contrary, I understand your pain and frustration. I just know how hard business is and how tough competition is. We're all ambassadors for our company, and the companies that customers want to do business with have people they can count on.

Being professional means putting on a brave face. Being employable means being a resilient team member who pushes through tough days because you are committed to your job, your coworkers, and your customers.

This isn't a new issue, but it's an important reminder that we have a job to do and we need to do the best we can when we can. And most of the time, we can.

Here's why you do it: First and foremost, we all have had bad days. But in this current culture of "authenticity" and "over-sharing," we sometimes fall back on that dynamic as permission to let it all show on our face and in our actions. *"I'm having a bad day. Okay? Get off my back!"*

But here's why we hate it: That. We don't need that in our face and we certainly don't appreciate your attitude, indifference, or distraction. We get that you've have a rough day. We have them too. But as customers we don't want to have to walk on eggshells, never knowing the kind of person we're going to encounter. We chose you, and in return we need our needs met, our calls returned, and a reasonable level of service. We can be patient to an extent, but keep in mind that we are paying for this.

Here's a better approach: When you're having a tough day (and who hasn't?) just look around at others around you and recognize that they might be having a tough day too. And in that moment, take a deep breath and make a decision that you're going to push through, put on a brave face, and not burden others with your troubles. People have their own stuff they're working through.

When we're all working to beat the competition, pay our bills, and feed our families, the best thing we can do to make it is to step up, do our job, and deliver an outstanding and consistent experience for our customers—regardless of what is burdening us.

Listen, you don't care that I have a cough. You care about your business. Do you know what? I care about your business too. That's why wrote this today.

CHAPTER 32

GET TO KNOW ME

By the time you are reading this chapter, you've gotten to know me pretty well. Through my lessons, stories, and assertions you probably have a pretty good sense of who I am and how I think. But how much do you really know about me? Perhaps you don't want to know more about me, and that's okay, but you should always want to know more about your customers. Let's discuss how a culture of curiosity can be a game-changer for your business.

Alignment In business is more important than ever. Aligning how we do business—how we offer, sell, and deliver our product or services—with the way our changing customers want to buy from us will determine the winners in this new normal. But creating alignment requires us to understand our customers on a deeper level—ideally, better than our competitors do.

Understanding and alignments is at the core of being customer-centric. It's a competitive advantage that comes from being more in tune with our customers, and then altering how we conduct business in ways that they prefer.

The truth is that our customers are more than simply their demographics and psychographics. They are real people, with rich, complex lives, fascinating and often unexpected back stories—just like the rest of us.

For example, you would likely not guess that as a kid, I struggled with an obvious speech impediment. I couldn't say my R's. I suffered all through elementary school. In fact, I would be pulled out of class for speech therapy three times a week for six years!

And it wasn't like I said: *"I want Wocky Woad ice cweam."* It was more subtle but certainly noticeable and I was teased mercilessly. Thewd gwade was a particular challenge for me.

Look at me today. I actually speak for a living. I teach and share and lead strategic meetings and retreats. I have spoken on some of the biggest stages for some of the biggest companies in the world.

Now, you might expect me to talk about the power of overcoming obstacles, or that this painful memory has fueled me for over 50 years. That I made a commitment to myself to prove to those bullies wrong! I'm going to show them!

But, no. It's hasn't. Ha! I hardly ever think about it. This isn't a story of "triumph over adversity." It's just... ironic.

Who would have ever imagined that I would end us as a verbal communicator? The kid who couldn't talk right now won't shut up! Kind of funny. But I'm not driven by that. It didn't define me. It's just... weird.

The point is that we think we know people, or we make assumptions, and then alter our behavior or approach based on what we assume. Or worse yet, we don't make any effort beyond the transaction itself. We think our job is to simply facilitate the transaction, deliver the report, or answer the phone, but it's more than that. Having a customer-centric mindset requires a measure of interest or curiosity about the person on the other side of the business relationship.

The truth is that people are interesting! Their stories are crazy, and their lives are often unexpected. Just what they've been through this week, would blow your mind! You are certainly complicated. Don't you think your customers are as well?

My great friend and colleague Jessica Pettit works with organizations to address and resolve issues surrounding inclusion and diversity. In her presentations, she notes that we all write a story in our mind about people when we meet them for the first time. It may or may not be a true story, but make no mistake, we all write one.

In fact, with her colorful hair and body covered in tattoos, people write stories in their mind about her the moment they see her for the first time. But as soon as she opens her mouth, you begin to recognize her brilliance.

> *"Our customers are more than simply their demographics and psychographics. They are real people, with rich, complex lives, fascinating and often unexpected back stories—just like the rest of us."*

Jessica taught social studies and has a master's degree in higher education administration. She creates curriculum and writes books, but you might not write *that* story in your mind when you first meet her.

She reminds audiences and organizations that when you write a story in your mind about who you believe someone is, be sure to leave a little room in the margins for "edits."

The point is that we need to *want* to learn more about our customers or clients. They have families and hopes and consternations and things that make them laugh, food that causes them digestive issues, or subjects they get emotional over. These are your customer, clients, vendors, constituents, partners, and co-workers. They are more interesting than you know.

Being customer-centric requires a mindset of "service empathy." It's easier to put yourself in their shoes—if you take a moment and put yourself in their shoes. This is not just about going through the buying process from their viewpoint, but taking a mental journey through their day. It's recognizing that their life might be very different than yours, and you should be curious about that.

Now to be clear, we most often don't, or even can't, know what their life is truly like. We don't really know what they go through on a day-to-day basis, but we can certainly recognize their humanity.

Just remind yourself that the person across from you, or on the phone, or on the Zoom call, is a complicated, interesting, and often wonderful person. Recognize that their humanity affects how we see them, and how we interact with them and serve them.

In a marketplace with no shortage of qualified competitors, a proven differentiator is better understanding your customers. Use that information and mindset to better align your policies, behaviors, and conversation to fit with what *they* identify with and find preferable.

Today, smart companies are less product-centric—where our expertise is in what we do—and are more about recognizing the power of being customer-centric. That shift requires curiosity that leads to service empathy.

Here's why you do it: We tend to put our head down and focus on our work and the task at hand. Our job is to do our job and we try to serve our customers and clients the best we can. That's the nature of business. We are busy and there are never enough hours in the day.

But here's why we hate it: Sometimes we wish you would just lift your head up and see us as more than simply another sale. I'm not suggesting that you are unfeeling or disconnected, but when you fail to really see us, you'll often miss the signs of our impatience or frustration, or fail to be empathic when we need you to understand that we want something different than what you're offering.

Here's a better approach: Look deeper at your best customers, or perhaps at your aspirational customers. Do some internet research on them and learn more about their lives. I'm not suggesting getting creepy. I'm saying you can learn a lot about people online.

How many of your best customers or clients have you ever tried to learn more about, perhaps their career and interests? Not everyone, but just some of them. What might you do differently based on what you learn about their background, family, hobbies, or career path?

When you get us, we feel it. When you see us, we feel seen and heard, and we're far more likely to feel connected and loyal to you.

The dictionary defines empathy as: *"The identification with, or vicarious experiencing of, the feelings, thoughts, or attitudes of another."* It's putting yourself in their shoes.

Service empathy is the ability to imagine the customer's journey from their perspective, and in doing so, delivering the experience—not that you want to offer—but one that they'd prefer to receive.

My job in these Huddle conversations is to be the voice of your customer. And it shouldn't matter if I can pronounce my R's correctly. But I can. Really. Just sayin'.

CHAPTER 33

WHO'S WAITING FOR YOU?

In business, we're often reminded to focus on our customers and give them our undivided attention. We're supposed to make them feel like the most important person in the room. Right? But what about the person standing behind them who is waiting for their turn? Are they less important? What about the person waiting for a response to their email or a returned phone call? Let's weigh-in on the complicated hierarchy of attention.

Early in my career, I will admit to being incredibly disorganized. I always took on way too many projects at work and important tasks would invariably fall through the cracks. I'm embarrassed to admit that I was so scattered that at 26 years old, my supervisor sent me to a two-day, time-management seminar put on by the creators of the Franklin DayTimer. Remember those notebooks? They made a popular day planner that helped you prioritize and schedule your day.

At the seminar, they reminded us that you couldn't just do the things you wanted do while letting other priorities slip. Everything had to be done. We learned how to consider all that was on our plate each day and rank them in order of importance.

The most valuable thing I learned, however, was how to recognize the difference between what was important and what was urgent. Having a client proposal due by the end of the day was certainly important, but the phone ringing was urgent.

So, how do we rank the *people* who need our attention? If more than one person wants access to you at the same time, how do you determine where to direct your attention? It could be a customer, but also a vendor, partner, or even a colleague.

We've all been there. Right? The easy answer is that the first attention goes to person in front of you, on the phone, or who texted first, but it's not that simple.

> "We need to adopt a clear service-empathy mindset and strategy that honors those in front of us, but also acknowledges those who are waiting for us."

It's a tough subject because we're trained and encouraged to give all of our customers our full attention and engagement. Perhaps a customer felt as if they waited a long time standing in line and now that they've reached the front they don't want to be rushed. But remember that others are often waiting as well. Do we ignore all of them in favor of the one who's in front of us?

Listen, we've all felt ignored by someone at a business at one time or another. Healthcare professionals struggle to balance this all the time. Their patient has been patient and wants time with the doctor or other provider to thoroughly address their concerns. Yet the doctor knows that someone else is waiting in the next room as well. Actually, the patient knows that too.

What about when you're on the phone with someone and a coworker stands in the doorway to your office with an impatient look because they have a time-sensitive question? You can't ignore one over the other. They're all important, right?

There's a tactical solution, of course. Simply acknowledging the person who is waiting and letting them know that you see them goes a long way. Pausing to verbally let them know that you'll be with them in a moment, or get back to them at a certain time, takes away much of the frustration of them feeling unseen.

But anything short of acknowledgment will fill those information gaps with negative scenarios in their own mind. They will ascribe dismissive feelings or attitudes to you that may not be true at all. When you're the customer and waiting for a businessperson to finish a call, or you're standing in a long line and the checker is casually talking with another customer about something random and they don't seem to recognize or care that others are waiting, we begin a dialogue in our mind.

"He knows I'm here, but he won't even look at me. Look at me. Look... at me!"

Or *"Yep. Just keeping chatting. Keep chatting Chatty Cathy. Oh, you just made a new friend didn't you? I'll just stand here for an hour while you learn everything about each other's hometown."* Grrrr.

Now, from the business perspective you're just trying to deliver great service and truly listen to your customer so that you can serve them best. You're not intentionally ignoring other people. You're with a customer! You'll be with them in a minute!

But did you say that out loud? Or did you say it with your eyes? We can't let people fall through the cracks because our attention is elsewhere. These other people are the lifeblood of our business.

Of course, this dynamic only grows as demands on our time and attention grows and our customers become more demanding. We need to adopt a clear service-empathy mindset and strategy that honors those in front of us—but one that also acknowledges those who are waiting for us.

And not everyone waiting for our attention is standing in front of us or in line. Some are simply waiting for a returned call, email, or an answer to a question or request. We have other priorities in front of us, but they don't know that—until they know it.

Once again, it's about acknowledgment of their presence and management of their expectations. People are generally reasonable provided they know that *we* know that they are waiting and understand how long the wait will be. In addition, this also gives them the opportunity to let us know if that doesn't work for them. And if not, we can work it out and come to a resolution.

This Huddle discussion isn't just about offering up an effective customer communication strategy. It's also an important reminder that we have to be sensitive too, not just to those in front of us but to those who are waiting for us.

Here's why you do it: We are only human, and we can only do one thing at a time. We have a client or customer or call, and we're trying to serve them and give them our attention. I get it. As customers we like it when we're being served well, so we try to deliver that level of service to our customers.

But here's why we hate it: If we're not the one being served, we don't want to feel ignored or less important to you. We need to know that you see us and will get to us—and when. When we're not recognized or addressed, we ascribe negative intent to that lack of attention. We feel disrespected or dismissed and that feels bad. Your customers feeling bad is very bad for business.

Here's a better approach: Turn your radar up a few notches and notice who is waiting for us. We know how it feels when we're on the other side of the equation.

In business, our current conversation can almost always survive a brief pause as we say: *"Forgive me for a quick moment"* and then turn our attention to others, letting them know that we appreciate their patience and that we will get to them momentarily.

In fact, our current customer will often appreciate the permission to fully engage with us without the pressure of knowing that others are waiting behind them.

As opposed to letting those emails go unanswered until we get around to it, we offer the sender a quick response letting them know that we got their message and that we'll give them a more thoughtful response before the end of the day or by the end of the week. We then need to put that task on our calendar so we can honor our word.

Listen, we all find ourselves on both ends of this dynamic. Sometimes we're the overwhelmed person being pulled in multiple directions, while other times we're the one waiting for a response or waiting for our turn.

To be clear, there are worse problems in business than having a long line of customers waiting to be served, but our job is to serve all of them and make all of them feel seen and heard. Some will be urgent to be sure, but they're all important.

CHAPTER 34

HAPPY TO SEE YOU

Have you ever noticed that we tend to like people who like us? I don't mean people who *are* like us, but people who actually like us. It's hard to not like them back. I want to talk about the profound effect of liking your customers and being grateful for their business, and the effect that has on their behavior.

When our daughter Sierra was little, she learned early on that the world was a very friendly place. Her mom would dress her up with little hats and headbands and bows. In fact, I don't think she ever left the house without something in her hair that perfectly matched the rest of her outfit.

Of course, people would smile and "ooh" and "ahhh" and make a big fuss over her. She saw nothing but smiles all day, every day, and it had a big effect on how she saw the world. To Sierra, people were always smiling, kind and friendly, and she responded in kind.

As a toddler, I remember she would confidently march 10 feet in front of us as we walked through the mall or at the park. She would smile and wave, saying, *"Hi," hi"* at everyone who walked by. It was hilarious. People would be taken aback by this confident little girl and of course they would smile and wave back. *"Oh, hi there!"*

To this day, now in her mid-twenties, Sierra is successful in her career as a digital media producer in Hollywood. Moreover, she is still that bright light with a positive spirit that people are just drawn to. She likes people and they certainly like her back.

Sierra learned a phenomenal lesson very early in life. It's the lesson espoused by a famous lyric in a wonderful song made popular by Louis Armstrong, *"When you're smiling, the whole world smiles with you."*

We are drawn to people with positive energy, and people like people that like them.

For those who are pet owners, you certainly know that profound excitement and love shown to you by your pet when you come home—even if you've only been gone for five minutes! Tail wagging and wet kisses and this unabashed excitement that says, *"I'm so happy to see you. I missed you! I love you!"*

> "There is something gratifying about supporting businesses with people who are likable and show us appreciation."

And what's our response? It's the same right back! *"Well, hi there. Yes. I know. I missed you too!"*

It's reciprocal. It feels good to know that someone likes you and missed you and is grateful for you.

It's the same in business. We know where we are welcome and appreciated—and we appreciate being appreciated.

Then again, we know when we're not, or when the other person is disinterested or disconnected. And while that's okay for the most part, it's certainly not preferable.

I was coaching a client recently and we were creating video messages for his business. In the middle of taping a segment I stopped and asked him if he was having fun. And he said, *"Yes." This is awesome!" "Then tell your face!"* I responded.

There is something apparent and visceral about knowing that someone is glad to see you, or happy to hear from you. You see it in their eyes and hear in their voice. It's authentic and magnetic. They like us, and we like people who like us.

Now, please don't dismiss that as simple Customer Service 101. *"Make sure you smile at everyone!"* That's not what I'm saying. I'm saying that authentic gratitude is tangible and is reflected in our behavior and attitude.

Do your customers know that you are grateful for their business? I guess a better question is: Are you grateful for their business? And not just the owners of your company, but everyone in the organization? Do you keep top of mind the reality that we exist, that we continue to operate profitably, only because our customers choose us over our competition?

My talented and elegant speaker colleague Lenora Billings-Harris shares about the African philosophy of *"Ubuntu."* Which loosely translated means: *"I am because we are,"* which is a simple way of saying that our individual identity comes through our collective humanity. That we exist and thrive because of our connection to others.

That's the essence of a successful business as well. Our recognition of the importance of the customers that we attract and serve, and the sense of connection that we foster, foretells our success. And that recognition, that gratitude, can make others feel welcome and appreciated. Without it, we fail to thrive.

In a competitive marketplace, who do you think is the preferred choice? Those who effectively sell to us and provide for us and deliver, install or ship to us? Or, those who do all of those things, but *also* get us, appreciate us, connect with us, and show it! Both are certainly competent and likely priced competitively, but there is something gratifying about supporting businesses with people who are likable and show us appreciation.

I think one of the most inspiring sentiments is a famous passage from Anne Frank's diary, where she writes: *"In spite of everything,*
I still believe that people are really good at heart."

Do you look at people that way? Despite our divisions and a contentious world, do you see others as good people, doing the best they can to support their families and live a meaningful life? I heard someone say once that *"every person in the world is the most important person in the world to someone."* See *that* person. The one who others like and love. There's a lot to like in most people, and if you take the time to see them and let them know how much you appreciate them and their business, you're more likely to like the person you discover—and they'll likely like you back.

> **Here's why you do it:** We don't often take the time to really get to know our customers, because there's often little time to get to know our customers. Work is called work for a reason and there's a lot of work to get done. Of course, we like our customers, but a higher level of connection is just impractical in most cases.

> **But here's why we hate it:** Okay, we probably don't hate it. But the opposite of love isn't hate. It's *indifference*. If we want to be more than effectively transactional, we have to be more than simply good at what we do. We have to be really good at making our customers feel welcome and appreciated.

> **Here's a better approach:** Look past the pressures of your day and consciously, intentionally see your customers as the complex, interesting, and human people that they are. Seeing something likable in people changes how we view them and that changes our approach and our behavior—even in subtle ways. That connection gets noticed and rewarded with similar feelings and repeat business.

> Making an organizational decision to overtly show appreciation to your customers isn't manipulative. It's just nice. Gratitude shows in your attitude. Making the effort to see people as good is a magnet for those who appreciate others who take the time to see them. And, of course, it makes everything better in your life as well. It makes for a better day.

My best days are when I get to talk with our daughter Sierra. I miss her and like her—a lot.

CHAPTER 35

CONVENIENCE ISN'T A STORE

If one of our most precious resources is time, then those things that impede on our time, or take extra time, costs us something that we value. In today's Huddle conversation I want to talk about how inconvenience alters how we see you, and how providing greater convenience can create a compelling competitive advantage.

When I grew up, it was a common practice to swing by the airport to drop off, or pick up friends and family. In fact, until 20 years ago, we could walk people all the way to gate and wave goodbye through the window. We'd even arrive early so we could greet loved ones as they got off the plane.

Today, the world is different. Not only is driving to the airport a big hassle, especially as I live almost an hour away from my home south of Denver, but the process itself is arduous. So when an out-of-state friend or business associate is flying into Denver, just swinging by the airport to pick them up can be hours out of my day. Then there's the sitting in your car in the off-site passenger waiting area or trying to anticipate the pickup time so you don't get busted for sitting too long outside baggage claim—and that's assuming there are no flight delays. Ugh.

Do you know what's really convenient? Uber and Lyft! Just having them jump in a ride-share car and covering the cost is super convenient—for both of us. How about calling a limo service and sending a driver to pick them up? That's a nice touch. Honestly, today it's not just nice, it's often a no-brainer.

Losing a half day of work is not a good option in most cases. Sure, sending a car to pick them up can be little pricier, but it's a price I am happy to pay because it frees up my most valuable resource: time.

Paying a premium for convenience is certainly not a new phenomenon. Think about: 7-11 or Circle K, Loaf N' Jug or Kwik Trip, or whatever serves your part of the world. It's no coincidence they're called "convenience stores." They're conveniently located on corners everywhere. They conveniently carry many of the most popular items for a quick grab and purchase while you're out. It's a quick and easy no-brainer.

> "When getting what we want from you is inconvenient or time-consuming, we look for alternatives."

But there is a tradeoff, isn't there? You'll pay more for a gallon of milk at a convenience store than you would at the full-service grocery store. That quart of motor oil, or box of emergency microwave popcorn, will set you back more than it would at a big box store.

The point is that we, as consumers, value convenience and are often more than willing to pay for it.

I speak and consult about the growing need to be remarkably easy to do business with. When you are seen as hard to do business with, it's likely because your process is unnecessarily complicated and time-consuming. How hard is it to buy your products, or to reach you, ask a question, customize the order, or get it delivered when we need it? Perhaps you force us to take on some of the process that we thought we were paying you for.

In short, our definition of "hard to do business with" is often a reflection of your level of inconvenience or refers to some bottleneck in your process creating a delay for us as customers.

Being easy to do business with is getting what we want quickly, shipped overnight, or delivered to our door, or your willingness to accommodate our small window of availability or your flexibility. Easy is when you offer to help us outside of working hours or on the weekend when it's more convenient for us. We like that a lot.

When getting what we want from you is inconvenient or time-consuming, we look for easier alternatives. Most of those options are likely a call or click away. But when you bend over backward to accommodate us, or simplify the process to make everything easier and faster, we see you as convenient. Translation: You are preferable.

Listen, there are thousands of examples of things that customers or clients find inconvenient, and just as many where the alternative is just the opposite—convenient!

The challenge is that too often the processes that companies put in place to create efficiency or predictability—to make things more convenient and predictable for their team members—conversely adds extra inconvenience to their customers.

So, when the staff at the airline counter at the airport is freed up from having to check you in or tag your luggage, it's only because they make us do it! While they stand by watching us do it, it's like we're paying them to supervise us so they don't have to do it—or pay someone on their team to do it!

When the receptionist or intake person at the medical clinic no longer fills in your personal information on that form, or has to enter it into the computer to check you in for your appointment, who do you think is expected to do it? Oh yeah, the sick or injured person—or their parents.

Just one more inconvenience in a growing list of duties shifted to us. My brilliant colleague and Customer Service guru, Shep Hyken, commissioned a study recently called *Achieving Customer Amazement* and the results were profound. The study showed that nearly 70% of people said flat out that would pay more for products or services that were more convenient for them. When he asked about delivery in particular, 90% said they would gladly pay more.

Do you know what's convenient? I can tell you: buying with one click, logging in with face ID, only having to give your personal information to the representative on the phone once—and not having to ask the same question or explain your issue over and over again with each new person you talk to in a string of redirected calls. "Let me put you in touch with someone who can help you," invariably means having to explain all over again what you just said to the previous person you spoke to!

Do you know what else is convenient? Having your groceries delivered, not having to pick up your dry cleaning, getting an automatic email when it's time to renew or reorder your meds, depositing a check by taking a picture of it with your phone and not having to drive to the bank. All wonderfully convenient!

There is a growing list of wonderful new conveniences that are reshaping customer behavior and expectations, and those changes are pulling us like a magnet from others who have yet to enhance their offering or simplify their process.

So, assuming your quality is top-notch—and it had better be—the real question today isn't about how good you are it's: How convenient are you?

Here's why you do it: We don't think we're inconvenient! Then again, who do you think created your process, products, and service delivery model? It's very effective for you. You designed it. Of course, it works—for you!

But here's why we hate it: We don't live in your world. Our days are different. Our life is different. We have things to do and so many choices of who to work with or buy from. Sometimes we just want to get in and out quickly and we want your process to be easy. In a competitive environment being better is important, but easy is better than better. Faster is better than better.

Here's a better approach: Examine every point along your customer's journey to identify hassles, bottlenecks, and delays. Better yet, walk that path with someone who doesn't know why you do it the way you do it and ask them what they find to be burdensome or inconvenient. Then take that point of contact or process and ask the question: What would make this more convenient for our customers?

Brainstorm ideas for rethinking processes with your team and ask them to create alternatives. My guess is that you'll get more great suggestions than you expect.

The dictionary defines *convenience* as: "*The state of being able to proceed with something with little effort or difficulty.*" Some might call that the definition of a no-brainer.

I would submit that the goal of a company with respect to their customers is to be thought of as a no-brainer. Being seen as a very convenient choice is a pretty good place to start. Just sayin.'

CHAPTER 36

FEELING CHEATED

Remember when you were a kid and somebody got something that you didn't get? It made you feel cheated and you cried, *"That's not fair!"* Then your parents would say something like: *"Well, sweetheart, life isn't fair."* Oh, that was so frustrating!

I want to talk about what happens when we feel cheated—and we feel it more often than we should.

When I was about 12 years old, I saw a commercial on TV for a set of record albums that featured dozens of the best songs of the year. That year was 1975, by the way.

The record featured popular songs like: "Sweet Home Alabama," "Boogie Down," and John Denver singing "Sunshine on My Shoulders." It was awesome! I had to have it.

Now, I was a music nut and I loved to buy and play my record albums, but I didn't always have a lot money. I was only 12. So, here was a two-record set that featured *60 Super Hits!* and it was priced the same as one regular record album.

So, for three weeks, I did all my chores and saved all my allowance money. I called the phone number from the TV commercial, gave them my money and then I waited, and waited—we had to wait in those days—for the records to arrive.

Two weeks passed, and the box finally came. My mom called to me from the kitchen and I ran downstairs to see her holding a thin, flat box with a big smile on her face. I knew exactly what was inside. I grabbed it from my mom, and I ran upstairs to my bedroom. I ripped open the packaging and pulled out this two-record set. I then lifted the top of my record player, dropped the record on the player and gently placed the needle on the outside rim. The first song began to play.

But something didn't sound right. So, I lifted the needle with my index finger, got down low to see the grooves and dropped it gently on the next song—and then the next. What the heck? The songs were familiar, but the voices were not. I grabbed the record jacket and looked closer, and there it was: *"Performed by the Realistics."*

It wasn't the original singers! Sixty of my favorite songs and they were all wrong! I had saved my money. I had waited two whole weeks. I had trusted them, and they tricked me! The record was horrible. It wasn't what I ordered. It wasn't what I wanted!

I was so upset that I slammed my door, threw myself on the bed, and I cried. I was only 12. In my mind, I had done everything right. I had spent my own money, but I didn't get what I paid for. I didn't get what I expected.

How often does that happen to us today? Not the crying part, but us feeling like we didn't get what we expected, or what we thought we were paying for? How often do we feel cheated—especially when ordering merchandise online?

Of course, it's rarely an intentional deception on the part of the business, but too often, when we have an expectation that isn't met, we feel as if we got ripped off, or we ascribe intent—like somebody did something *to us* by not doing enough *for us*.

When the food comes out at a restaurant and the portion size is really small, we feel cheated. When we order something from the internet and it arrives looking nothing like the photo, or the quality is terrible, we feel like we got suckered. When we can't get cell phone coverage near our home or office, we feel like we're getting charged for a cell phone that we can't even use!

The fact that the policy might be spelled out clearly, or included in the fine print, is irrelevant. When we feel like we paid for something or believe we were promised something and we don't get it, or get something different, or get it late, or don't get enough of it—we feel taken. We feel cheated.

And regardless of the intent, you are left with an unhappy customer. Too often, the person assigned to deal with that person had no role in the perceived offense, but they are left to clean up the mess.

> **"For every dissatisfied person that you hear from, bet on a dozen more who never said a word."**

So, of course, we craft that script: *"I'm so sorry that happened to you Mr. So and So. I know how frustrating that must be."*

Listen, I have no problem trying to make sure your customers know that you understand what they must be going through, but the more important thing is what happens when you move past the script to finding a resolution that addresses their unique scenario.

Chatbots, FAQs, and other automated detours were created to offload common issues to free up your team and your time. Honestly, I think those are relied upon far too often. The real challenge is the "F" in the "FAQ." What if the question isn't "frequently" asked, or frequently dealt with? What if you didn't do anything wrong, but your customer just didn't understand?

In business, however, perception is reality, and most often customer concerns are not a one-off. If a client or customer misinterpreted your offer or claim, or assumed something about your policy or product, you can bet that others probably do as well.

For every dissatisfied person you hear from, bet on a dozen more who never said a word. They just didn't come back.

Today, when we feel as if your offer is misleading, or that you are being less than responsive when we express a concern, or a technician didn't arrive in the promised appointment window, we don't slam the door and cry on our bed. We go online and we tell... everyone. Some people will keep telling everyone who will listen until they feel like you are listening and making some effort to make it right.

The point is that you need to look at your promises—which is everything you offer, produce, deliver, install, cook, repair, or sell. When you take someone's money, you've made a promise. Just make sure both of you are in agreement as to what is being sold and what's being bought.

Here's why you do it: Most often we live with our products and services every day. We're immersed in it. It's our life, or at least 40 hours of it every week (at least). What is there to misunderstand? It's right there, clear as day.

But here's why we hate it: We have our own idea of what we think we are buying or ordering. Most often it's based on expectations based on past buying experiences, or because we see the picture on your website or in your promotion. We see a picture of either the product itself or the happy person enjoying it. We expect *that*. When we don't get *that* we feel cheated, and we don't like feeling cheated and we don't like those who we feel cheated us.

Here's a better approach: Look and listen. Look at your products or process from the customer's perspective. Are you delivering what you would expect if you were a customer ordering it or buying for the first time?

Then, don't stop listening to comments or complaints. Don't be defensive. And after making it right with them, consider if you would feel the same if you were them. That's called "service empathy."

Is their concern valid? Could your offer be misinterpreted, or did your delivery underwhelm your customer? Don't hesitate to change or adjust something in your business model or promotion to create clarity of expectation. In fact, it should be an ongoing effort.

And in case you were wondering, the answer is "no." My parents didn't reimburse me for what I spent on that stupid record. And "no," I never made that mistake again. It was a painful lesson, and "yes," thinking about it still makes me angry—45 years later.

CHAPTER 37

BEING REMARKABLE

In business, we all know the importance of building your brand. Of course, your brand isn't just your logo, it's your entire reputation. It's everything that people think about when they think about you. And while we have no control over what people think, we do have great influence. Let's talk about your role in influencing how your customers think about you and the brand you're building.

I overheard a conversation recently between my two daughters; both are in their 20s. Actually, I only heard one side of the conversation, as they were talking on the phone and one of them was in the same room with me. I heard my one daughter say to the other: *"Well, you know how Dad is,"* as she looked over at me and rolled her eyes.

"Wait. How Dad is?" I asked. Of course, she waived me off with a dismissive gesture and went back to her conversation.

And it got me thinking about how Dad is? How am I?

The more interesting thing is that they both knew exactly what she was talking about without actually detailing it. Together, they had a shared experience growing up with me as their father.

Alright, I get that. I am who I am, and I acknowledge that I parent the way I parent—to them and to their brother and later, to their stepsiblings as well. As a result, they have a shared impression of how Dad is.

Now to be clear, I am a very intentional parent. I'm not saying I'm harsh by any means, but I did make a commitment to help raise, loving, responsible, healthy, and self-confident people who make a contribution to this world. I did that with a million hugs, 20 million kisses, and way too many life lessons, which they would probably call "lectures"—because I'm a talker. No surprise.

My intention and behavior have always been in pursuit of those noble ends. Over the years, those actions—combined with my human faults—built my reputation with my kids, and how they talk about me to each other.

My question for you is: What reputation are you building? How do people talk about you and your business? Beyond the basic competence required of all businesses, and the ethical mandate to do the right thing, do people know you and talk about in a way that is flattering?

I guess, more importantly, do people talk about you in the way that you want them to talk about you? I'm not talking about whether they know your slogan or can sing your jingle, but do they describe you in terms that recognize what makes you special, different, and preferable over others who do what you do?

Seth Godin was an early influencer of mine, and he wrote about the importance of being "remarkable" in the sense of being worthy of being remarked about.

So, what makes you worthy of conversation? What is special about your business, products or approach, and how do you demonstrate that "specialness" to your customers and clients consistently? Is there a consensus among your team as to the reputation you are working to build?

And just like I have been with my kids, do you have the end in mind? Does everyone across your company know what behavior they need to consistently demonstrate to achieve the reputation you desire? Are you all on the same page?

Here's a great exercise to do with your team:

Ask everyone to identify their favorite company or brand and list five words that describe that company—five attributes that come to mind when they think of that business or product.

For example, Apple might bring to mind words like innovative, easy to use, cutting-edge, cool, and expensive. Whole Foods might make you think healthy, unique choices, fresh, free delivery, and gluten-free or natural.

> "Is there a consensus among your team members as to the reputation you are working to build?"

Now, have your team think about your company and ask: What are five words or five descriptions that we should aspire to? One year from now, if we were to ask our customers or prospects to describe us, what do we want them to say? What are five things we want everyone to think of at the mention or our name?

Then ask the most important question: What do we need to do every day between now and one year from now to build that reputation, and what behavior or distractions might get in our way?

What are the extra efforts, the less-divided attention we give our customers, the more interest we can pay in them? What are the new policies, offerings, or accommodations that would help us to be thought of, not just as a good choice but as a better choice? Write it all down, discuss it, and come to consensus. Then, come to an agreement as to what we will all do differently.

To be clear, that mindset as well as all of those behaviors aren't necessarily intuitive. Often, they are the result of intentionality—making a conscious, organizational decision to be remarkable—to be worthy being remarked about.

I love doing this work with organizations, to spark discussion, and get them thinking and brainstorming as a team. Who are we? What believe and what behavior do we need to demonstrate so that others see it, feel it, and remember it?

This is a lot more than simply crafting and displaying your company mission statement—although that can be important start. We can't assume that everybody in our company knows how we want to be thought of.

Of course, we certainly assume everyone understands their job, but the question is: Does everyone in your company know their role?

Here's why you do it: Focusing on our job and doing a good job is at the core of keeping our job. But I would submit that without a clear understanding of what we want our customer to feel, believe, and remember about us, we lack the context to really understand why we've been asked to do our job. The definition of doing a good job for our company also has to include becoming who our customers prefer.

But here's why we hate it: As customers what we hate is inconsistency. When there's a lack of consensus as to how you want us to feel when doing business with you, what you generally get is a really good company who delivers well, most of time. But you're also missing the opportunity to be better than that.

Here's a better approach: Put your heads together and have a conversation, not just about what you do, but what you want your clients and customers to remember after doing business with you. Commit specific expectations and behaviors to writing and agree that each person across the company will deliver that consistently. I promise you, that consistency will pay off.

A famous quote (that's been attributed to a variety of people) says: " would worry far less about what people think about you if you knew ¹e they actually do."

don't generally think about us or talk about us. They have But building your business and building your brand ople something to talk about.

And I don't mean to sound like a broken record, but... well, you know how Dad is.

CHAPTER 38

WHAT YOU THINK YOU KNOW

I want to talk about what you think you know. When we're having a conversation with someone and there's a voice in our head that says, *"Okay, get on with it,"* it's often because we already know where this is going, and we already know what they are going to say, and all this "fluff" is just wasting time. But is it? I want to highlight the dangers of believing what you know—or what you think you know.

I was having an odd issue with my office Wi-Fi recently and needed to call my Web services provider. Without getting into specifics, I was struggling with a very frustrating, but somewhat unusual and unique technology issue.

So I called the customer service line, and after a full 20 minutes sitting on hold, the representative answers the call and asks for my account information to verify my identity, which I provided. Then he asks how he can help me.

I begin to explain my issue, but after only 10 seconds, he interrupts me and starts going into his scripted speech about Wi-Fi speeds and what they cannot guarantee. But that wasn't the issue I was dealing with, and I wasn't done explaining my situation.

So I begin to explain again, and *again* he starts to talk over me explaining their policy. Now we are both talking at the same time.

So what do I do? I talk louder and I'm not pausing because I don't appreciate him talking over me, because I had been waiting on hold for 20 minutes, and I have this recurring issue to discuss and I am working in my office and I don't have time for this!

But he just keeps talking! I'm getting furious with his audacity, and then I realize... that it's a recording. I'm battling with a recorded message and I'm oscillating between feeling really stupid and feeling frustrated that I got stuck having a conversation with a computer "guy" attempting to help me with my issue, but of course, he doesn't even really understand my issue—because he's not even real!

So, I mutter something about hating robots and I start repeating: "*Real person! Real person!*" into the phone hoping that this artificial "intelligence" will recognize the command and redirect me.

But to my surprise, the voice one the other end of the phone says: "*Sir, I am a real person.*"

Stunned, I say: "*Oh...sorry, I thought you were a computer voice. You kept talking at the same time as me and I assumed you weren't real. I'm really sorry.*"

"*So anyway, here is my issue...*" And he starts talking again!

At this point, I had enough of this and said, "*Hang on! You keep talking over me. My challenge is...*"

And he interrupted once again and said: "*Sir, if you would let me finish...*"

And I said: "*No sir, you need to let me finish! I called you and I'm trying to explain the issue that I'm having so you can then give me your response and help me resolve it.*"

He let out a big sigh and said very sarcastically: "*Go ahead.*"

Okay, understand—I'm now speaking to you, the reader—that I pay nearly ten thousand dollars a year to this company for all my office services. I'm not a hassle. I'm their customer! Now, I'm sure he gets tired of talking to frustrated people all day—but he's in technical support! His job is to help people who are frustrated.

But instead of "*going ahead*" as he was allowing me to do, I asked to speak to a supervisor. Then he had the gall to say: "*Sir, a supervisor is going to tell you the same thing.*"

"How do you know what they're going to say?" I responded, clearly frustrated. *"You don't even know what my issue is. You think you know, but I haven't even had the chance to complete a sentence because you're so determined to read your script. I'll wait for a supervisor. Thank you!"*

He sighed again and put me on hold. The rest of the story is fairly uneventful. I did get the issue resolved. It was fairly straightforward for someone who took the time to listen to my question and fully understand my issue.

> **"I promise you that the scripted response you want to deliver is not nearly as important as the unique issue your customer wants to discuss."**

Now, I recognize that most business scenarios don't escalate to this degree, but many situations certainly have that potential. When a customer feels as if they aren't being listened to, you don't know what might happen next. The disconnect and frustration lived in that gap between what I wanted to explain and what he *thought* I was going to say. To be fair, in most cases we do have a pretty good idea of someone's question or issue before they finish it because so many of us have dealt with hundreds of scenarios and answered just as many questions. But that's not the point.

People want to be heard. They want to *feel* heard. It doesn't matter if you're in health care, auto repair, food service, logistics, or technology, every situation has the potential of being unique and even complicated. So, we have to take a moment to listen and not just quickly respond.

I used to lead meetings with CEO roundtable groups, and we had a powerful way of "issue processing" with our group members to help them address some of their most pressing business challenges.

Here's how it worked: A CEO member would have a business or even personal issue to raise with their colleagues in the group. After explaining the challenge they were facing, they would then have to ask a very specific question of the group like: *"How do I best deal with__?"* or *"I'm wondering what I should I do about__?"*

Of course, these were very smart people sitting around the table and an answer would quickly pop into the mind of each one of them. However, they weren't allowed to offer up that answer. They were only allowed to ask what we called "clarifying questions" to better understand the issue. What other factors were involved? What they had tried before? Why is solving this important to them, etc. Sometimes the group members would ask questions for over 20 minutes before they were allowed to offer a single solution.

That time, dedicated to information-gathering, helped to generate far better, far more informed and specific answers than the knee-jerk ones they would have happily given immediately after the issue was raised. The answers were always better because they better understood the question and the dynamics that led to it.

The point is that we're all smart people. We know what we're doing because this is what we do. But don't be so quick to assume that you know what your customers want and need. Listen first. Don't just wait for them to finish. Really listen and consider. I promise that your answers will be better, and your customers and clients will be grateful for the respect that you've shown them.

Here's why you do it: Honestly, it's just a matter of time. We don't always need to listen to the same questions or a story we've addressed so many times before. If we've got an easy and ready answer to quickly solve their issue, that's what our customers want. Right?

But here's why we hate it: No. It's not right. You don't know our question. You just think you do. (Okay, maybe you do, but then again, maybe you don't.)

When you jump in with your answer, or worse, say "no" to your customer before fully considering their situation and whether or not you could say "yes," it's just frustrating. We need you to listen first. Our situation might be unique, or we might need a unique solution or accommodation. When you're too eager to help, or too rigid in your scripted response to listen, you will likely frustrate your customers.

Here's a better approach: Be conscious of the tendency to jump in on others' questions with your solutions. Your customers want to be heard, and you need to hear them.

There is a great line that says: *"The opposite of talking isn't listening. It's waiting to talk."* Don't wait for your turn to talk. Listen to what your customers or clients are asking for. It may be different than what you think!

As important as your well-crafted response to your frequently asked questions may be, legally or otherwise, try using that scripted response only when you need to, and you might not need to, if you take a pause to truly understand the issue or questions they have.

I promise you that the scripted response you want to deliver is not nearly as important as the unique issue your customer wants to discuss.

I know. I'm that customer, and oftentimes, you are too. Just sayin'.

CHAPTER 39

CROSS TRAIN YOUR PEOPLE

How many people in your company know what you do? I'm not just speaking to the company leaders, but to all of you. If you were to quit, become ill, or take an extended leave of absence, would others be able to step in and assume your role? In this Huddle conversation, I want to talk about the critical importance of knowing more about others' roles and responsibilities.

When my middle daughter, Sydney was about twelve years old, she was very into basketball. Every weekend and many weeknights, I drove her to basketball practice or games at one of the local middle schools or high schools.

But on far too many occasions, all of the parents and kids would be left standing outside the school freezing in the frigid Colorado air because nobody had bothered to show up with the keys to the school gym. The school itself was always locked after hours, but we were supposed to be able to go in through the gymnasium's outside door. Even the referees would be stuck outside freezing as they tried calling the emergency phone numbers in their district supplied binders, because the one person that was entrusted with the keys to the gym had overslept, or couldn't be reached. One person!

Where was the backup? Who else could we call? We were freezing, and this happened at least a dozen times over the years. It just always seemed ridiculous to me and everyone else, that we couldn't get into the building where basketball games had been on the schedule for months.

In your company, is there only one person assigned to every job? Is there more than one person with the skills to do that thing you do? There was a time when everyone could do everything. Right?

Ask any group of four year olds how many of them can sing, and every hand will shoot high into the air. Ask them how many of them can dance. Once again, all the hands will be raised high and giggles will fill the room. A few of them will likely leap to their feet and start doing an impromptu dance to the delight of all those around them. It's what they do. They're four!

But ask those same questions to a room full of high school seniors and most won't move a muscle, shooting nervous glances at the others in the room. A few might raise their hand sheepishly, while others will simply point at those who are known for being talented singers or dancers.

It's all a reflection of their motivation and internal drivers. Young kids want to have fun and feel included, while teenagers have a profound aversion to judgment and ridicule.

As we get older, we do tend to gravitate toward the things that we're good at. Much of that narrowing from generalist to specialist is preparation for our work life. When we begin to recognize what we're good at, what we enjoy, it sets the stage for our early career choices.

But what happens when we're needed to perform other duties at work, and not just the things that fit within our job description? What if budget challenges, company layoffs, pandemics or even rapid growth leaves positions unfilled, people working off-site, or coworkers feeling overwhelmed? Who's there to step up and help?

Of course in the not-for-profit world, they just call this Tuesday. Every day their team has to do more with less. As a not-for-profit, whether a charity, professional association or advocacy group, they are always scrapping for the funds needed to fulfill their mission. Staff is a luxury and well-paid staff is almost unheard of. Everyone has to do everything.

How many jobs could you do in your company? If the pandemic taught us anything, it's that we have to be nimble. We have to do more and know more, because the person who knew and did that specific function, or used to answer that question, may be working from home, or might no longer be working for the company at all.

Think about you customers or clients calling for information, or needing an answer to a question, or a problem solved or trouble-shot. How do they feel when you don't know the answer and need to be handed off again and again to find someone who does? Better yet, how do you feel when you're passed off to another, or placed on hold for the third of fourth time?

> *"Pull back the curtain and let your people, (or your person) know how we make money, what vendors we work with, and how we keep the lights on."*

When your organization is overly-siloed and your team members only really know what they know and what they do, you're setting the stage some potentially frustrated customers and unreasonably long delays in getting them what they want.

Listen, I realize that the notion of cross-training has been around for a long time, but we've also seen a shift in recent years to over-specialization among professionals and the creation of "centers-of-excellence" within organizations. We want the best of the best, and assessments like Strengthfinders, Myers Briggs and others, help us to put the best people in the right seats on the bus.

But we've also see what happens when the bus driver gets sick, we get a flat tire or have engine trouble. Someone has to fix that tire, or drive the bus to the next stop. Who's going to be that person, if that person isn't there?

We are knee-deep in uncertain times. No longer can we count on next year unfolding the same as last year. Being nimble, isn't just being flexible with work schedules and locations, but also being prepared for curveballs that require others to step up to the plate and assume additional duties.

If we are to own our customers' problems, we each have to know more about our company, how it works and the processes we follow. It's not just who does what job, but what specifically is the job that they do?

These are very uncertain times to be sure, and with everything you have to deal with, make sure you aren't caught off-guard looking for the person who knows the answer, or the one person with the keys to the high school gym.

Here's why you do it: We get a bit siloed and job-specific because the jobs today are frankly more complicated then they were in yesteryear. Competitors are better, customers are more demanding and the work is just harder. Of course we need the best people doing the right jobs.

But here's why we hate it: We don't know your org chart. We just have questions we need answers to or issues we need to have resolved. We don't know the right person to go to, or ask. In fact, we want YOU to be the right person. And we certainly don't want to be told that so-and-so is off today, working from home, or get passed along again and again. It's frustrating.

Here's a better approach: Find a way for everyone to know something about everything—or at least a lot more than they do about other roles. Put formal programs and processes in place to allow for cross training and cross learning.

There are well-established programs like job shadowing and employee orientation videos that break down each of the departments and the role they play in the company's success.

And even if you're a very small company, pull back the curtain and let your people, (or your person), know how we make money, what vendors we work with, and how we keep the lights on. It will safeguard your company against the next pandemic or even a key staff member's unexpected departure.

And before we finish, I have two final questions: So, who can sing? And... who can dance?

CHAPTER 40

PLAYING THE LONG GAME

It's a general rule that older generations will complain about the younger ones. *"Kids these days!"* Whether it's their terrible music, their head-scratching fashion, or their head buried in their electronic devices, it's hard to keep our mouth shut sometimes.

But there's one specific mindset today that is too often celebrated and encouraged. It's a dangerous mantra that can lead to some very bad personal and business decisions.

As the father of five kids and stepkids, the youngest of whom is currently 17 years old, I'm not out of touch. Trust me, I've been doing this for a long time, thank you very much. But staying connected to their world is essential if I'm to help guide them and give them important perspective. I'm well acquainted with LOL, BTW, IDK and most other texting acronyms. (That's how cool I think I am.) But it's YOLO that really bothers and concerns me.

Listen, every generation has their version of *You only live once.* It's an encouragement to be bold, go after what you want, and live life to its fullest. I get it. But today, there seems to be a growing feeling of uncertainty regarding the future that's fueling this mantra of *"Be happy now 'cause tomorrow may not come."* That concerns me, and it should concern you as well.

My wife and I were having a conversation recently with a young couple. The young woman in the couple was the daughter of some very close friends of ours, and she her boyfriend had been dating for a few months. She was three years into college, but he had taken a different route, which is certainly his choice. What bothered her parents—*a lot*—was that he was encouraging her to drop out of college to go on adventures, or whatever he had in mind. Her parents asked us to talk with them.

As we talked, the overconfident young man was attempting to make the case for her abandoning her degree program, and then these ignorant words came out of his mouth: *"Hey, life is short."*

To which I responded: *"Friend, I know everyone says that, but it's a load of garbage. Life isn't short. Life is long!*

At 21 years old, you've just completed the shortest season of your life. You have a long, long life ahead of you if you're lucky, and the decisions you make today will affect the quality of that life for the next 60 or 70 years. The job you'll have, the income you'll earn, the success of your relationships, and the longevity of your body all depend on making good choices—today!

Life is long. It can be wonderful, but it can also be hard. Bad decisions make life much, much harder than it has to be."

The point I was making was that we need to avoid making short-term decisions based on instant gratification. In life and in business, we need to play the "long game." We need to have an extended vision of where we want to go and who we want to be along that journey.

Let me be more specific in terms of how that applies to our business: Everything we do contributes to our brand: our reputation in the marketplace, every success we earn and every time we fall short, every thrilled customer as well as those we've disappointed along the way. The decisions we make, the words we say, and how we behave toward our customers affects the reputation we are building.

But our brand is also every competitor that we disparaged in an attempt to make ourselves look better in comparison. It's the decision to give our customers a little bit less so we can keep a little more, and how they feel about that.

It's our decision to respond to a social media post from someone who disagrees with us about politics or some other issue because we know that we're right and we can't resist the urge to make sure they know that they're wrong! It's a short-term dopamine fix that doesn't serve anyone in the long run. Yeah, you certainly told them!

> "A long view in business leads to well-considered strategies instead of merely fast-facilitated transactions."

Having a mindset of "life is short" or "you only live once" in the best of scenarios encourages people to take risks and build a business, or a pursue a life that you're passionate about. But in the worst cases, it becomes an excuse to look for shortcuts as we chase quick success hits at the expense of long-term reputation or future opportunities.

I know a guy who planned on quitting his job to just travel for a couple of years in an RV. Sounds fun, right? But prior to that move, he planned on intentionally "working the system," as he described it. He was going to apply for a bunch of credit cards, charged them all up, get a ton of "free stuff," as he put it, and then file for bankruptcy. He stance was: *"Hey, life's short and those companies can afford it."* To be clear, he's not my friend. Just a guy.

That short-term gratification, in his mind, justified his astonishingly unethical behavior. The truth is that the YOLO mindset is far more prevalent today than most people recognize. But building a business, an ethical, sustainable, and preferable business, requires a long view and behaviors that support it. Customers are watching. The marketplace is watching.

In fact, every interaction with our customers has to be mindful of the lifetime value of that customer and the impact of a negative experience or a negative perception. Every conversation and transaction needs to recognize its impact on our reputation.

Listen, I have no issue with creative and even aggressive business strategies that go after customers, change the paradigm, or even disrupt categories. In fact, that's not really chasing short-term gain, it's often accelerating innovation and driving new sales and success—but it's not at the expense of relationships and reputation.

A long view in business leads to well-considered strategies instead of merely fast-facilitated transactions. A long view fosters clarity of brand, integrity and even our intentional collective company culture. We may live only once, but if we're smart, our business life can be nearly as long as our actual life.

Here's why you do it: There's a cultural mindset today that teaches that happiness is something that we go after, as opposed to the result of the work we do, the people we meet, and the relationships we foster. In fact, many people believe that those who wait to be happy, or have to work for it, are suckers. Go after it! Grab it! Take what makes you happy. You only live once, right?

But here's why we hate it: As customers, we notice when we're being offered less or when you've skimped on quality so you can save money. We see the stories of people who made money on insider trading or scammed customers or investors.

When companies take shortcuts, it often backfires. When a business fails to take responsibility for a defective product, or make things right when things go wrong, or makes it difficult to get a refund when it's due, we know that you've opted for short-term revenue over long-term relationships and success.

Here's a better approach: Be very clear on the long-term vision for your business. What products, services, approaches, behaviors, and even conversations might affect that vision you have?

Of course, not all business decisions or interactions are black and white, but there is a distinction between behavior that merely leads to short-term gain and those strategies that support long-term success. Ideally, they're both in play. When they aren't, bad things can happen. Often, you'll know it by the customers who leave and don't come back.

In short, my advice to business leaders and their teams is the same advice my mom and dad gave to me. It's that same advice I give my kids every time they walk out the door: Make good choices.

CHAPTER 41

ONE YEAR FROM NOW

Can you remember your life one year ago today? The world has changed to be sure, but have you? What have you learned over the past year and what are you doing differently today as a result?

In this book's final Morning Huddle conversation, I'd like to offer a unique perspective on growth and what that means for both your customers and your business.

One of my heroes in the speaking business was a remarkable man named Charlie Jones. Most people knew him as Charlie "Tremendous" Jones. At well over six feet tall, he was a bigger-than-life character with the onstage charisma and big personality of a southern preacher.

When people asked him how he was doing, he would answer *"Tremendous!* "in a big booming voice. Business audiences loved him. In fact, everyone loved him—and he loved them back.

His book *Life is Tremendous* has sold millions of copies and has been published in 12 languages around the world. Charlie practiced what he called "hugging therapy." In fact, he claimed to have hugged between 100 and 300 people every day! When he met you, he would give you this giant embrace, and just as you began to let go, to release the hug, you realized that he wasn't letting go.

"Oh, okay. I guess we're still doing this," you'd think to yourself. And what began to get a little awkward, quickly became welcome, as you'd just relax into this bear hug. He was warm and comforting in a gentle grandfatherly way.

You knew he wasn't doing it for affect. He genuinely liked people, and his message and bravado and enthusiasm for people made him one of a kind. He passed away a few years ago, and I was blessed to know him and be on the receiving end of some of those big bear hugs.

Among the countless words of wisdom Charlie delivered from the stage and in his writing was an assertion that has given me pause on many occasions. He famously said: *"You will be the same person in five years as you are today except for two things: the people you meet and the books you read."*

Charlie was a fierce proponent of reading and even created his own book company to promote his business books and those of others. I've come to recognize that what he was saying was that we need to keep learning, and we have to keep cultivating and nurturing new relationships. At its core, everything about this Morning Huddle initiative is about those two things: Ongoing learning about new ways to serve our customers, and the importance of fostering and solidifying new relationships with our customers, clients, and coworkers. It makes them feel connected enough to share positive comments about us. And most importantly, what we learn will stay with us and come back to us.

Customer experience is all about the relationships we have with our customers and the ones that they have with us. And not to get overly touchy-feely, but everyone wants to feel connected to something, or some things or people, causes, and community.

But we can also feel connected to brands, businesses, fashion, and vendors that feel like... us. *That's* where I like to shop! Or what my look is, the food that I prefer, or the people I want to give my business to because they've always been fair and treat me well.

At the end of the day, our business survival and profitability are dependent upon attracting and retaining our tribe. We are the right choice for them, and they like us.

If you want to see a connection between a business and their people— their tribe, just walk around Whole Foods for an hour, or a Harley Davidson dealership, Cracker Barrel, or Planet Fitness. These brands are magnets for *their* people.

Of course, we certainly want to cast a wide net and attract as many followers or customers as we can, but as for the core of our business, the only reason we survive is because of our ideal customers, core audience, and tribe. They know us, like us, feel connected to us, and are well served by us.

Where I will differ from Charlie Tremendous Jones is that I believe that five years from now you will not be the same person or the same company if you don't also change and adapt. In fact, you will likely be far behind and falling further and further behind every day.

If you aren't learning, growing, changing, and finding new and creative ways to connect with your customers, align with your clients, understand how much is constantly changing in their world, and taking steps to change along with them, you will be left behind by others who have made learning and changing a priority.

We started together on this journey on page one. Perhaps that was a few days ago, or maybe many months ago depending on how you approached this book. And as a little reminder, over the course of this book we have covered:

- The importance of *gifting* people your undivided attention.
- Recognizing how often we say *"no"* to our customers, and how to shift that mindset to: *"Let me tell you what I can do."*
- We've learned how we can future-proof our business by pretending to compete against ourselves.
- How to fire customers when we need to—and doing so in a manner that doesn't create bigger problems for them and us.
- The importance of setting aside time and teams to focus on solving problems and creating innovative programs and initiatives.
- What happens when we cross that conversation line and make things uncomfortable.
- Why we can never let all things be equal in the minds of our customers.
- How to make sure your customers never feel cheated, or like they've received less than they expected.
- The importance of playing the long game to create a powerful, preferable, and sustainable business.

- How to create an army of ambassadors that sing your praises.

Of course, we covered many other subjects as well to remind you to look at your business and the buying process from your customer's perspective.

Writing this book and the video series that spawned it, has been one of the most rewarding journeys of my career—and that journey is ongoing. The process has pushed me to learn more, think harder, and remain focused on delivering real, actionable content for you and your team.

The second "season" of lessons and conversations is already in the works with new subjects, cautionary tales, insights, and actionable lessons to make you think. More importantly, the goal is to keep you and your team talking about what each subject means to you and your business—and then to take action as a result.

The content and ideas may come from me, but the answers and the actions are always up to you.

And because this is how I wrap up all my huddle conversations:

Here's why you do it: We learn, grow, and work to foster strong relationships with our customers because that's what it takes to survive and thrive in today's complex business world. Full stop.

But here's why we hate it: We sometimes hate it because it's hard work. If it were easy, everyone would do it well—and they don't. But you can. It's hard, but it's worth it.

Here's a better approach: Never stop learning. Never stop talking and challenging each other and your assumptions about how you do things today. Stay tuned in to the changing needs, wants, and expectations of your customers and clients.

Customer experience is not a one-time presentation, conversation, or even a book. It's an ongoing journey and a relentless quest for service excellence. I hope you'll stay with me on that journey. We've got big plans for new Huddle conversations!

It has been a remarkable and sometimes exhausting year to create all these conversations, and I'm grateful that you've come on this journey with me.

In fact, I wish I could give each of you a hug—a big, lingering, slightly awkward, holding on a little too long, Tremendous hug.

Thank you!

ABOUT THE AUTHOR

David Avrin, CSP, Global Speaking Fellow, is the President of The Customer Experience Advantage, a strategic consultancy based in Castle Rock, Colorado. David is a popular keynote speaker, strategic facilitator, and business consultant. He has presented for audiences and worked with organizations across America and in dozens of cities on six continents around the world including: Singapore, London, Bangkok, Sydney, Barcelona, Mumbai, Abu Dhabi, Buenos Aires, Belfast, Manila, Johannesburg, Monte Carlo, Toronto, New Delhi, Dubai, and more.

His insights on competitive advantage have been featured on hundreds of television programs and podcasts and in thousands of online and print publications around the world.

David Avrin offers high-content, engaging, entertaining, and interactive presentations and strategic sessions on Customer Experience as a marketable competitive advantage to help organizations better understanding their changing customers and future-proof their business.

He is the host of The Customer Experience Advantage Podcast which can be heard on most major podcast platforms including: C-Suite Radio, Apple Podcasts, Spotify, Stitcher, and more. The video version of the podcast is available on David Avrin's website and YouTube Channel.

Connect with David Avrin on all social media outlets as "David Avrin." (On Instagram as "@TheRealDavidAvrin.")

David lives happily with his wife and family in the Denver suburb of Castle Rock, Colorado.

Working with David Avrin

To learn more about bringing David Avrin in to speak or consult with your organization, visit: www.DavidAvrin.com

Email David Avrin at info@DavidAvrin.com

To watch a preview video of David's in-person and virtual presentations, visit: www.DavidAvrinPreview.com. You will see in a few short minutes why David Avrin is one of the most popular business speakers in the world today!

The Customer Experience Advantage Morning Huddle Video Series is a done-for-you internal engagement initiative where David Avrin leads your Morning Huddle meeting each week. It includes a weekly video message and facilitator's guide with a Huddle introduction and even sample questions to keep the conversation going. Learn more about bringing this powerful and very affordable initiative to your team at www.CustomerExperienceAdvantage.com

Also by David Avrin

Why Customers Leave (and How to Win Them Back)
(Career Press 2019)

Visibility Marketing
(Career Press, 2016)

It's Not Who You Know, It's Who Knows You!
(Originally published by John Wiley & Sons, 2009; 2nd edition, Classified Press, 2014)

The 20 Best and Worst Questions Reporters Ask
(Classified Press, 2009)

The Gift in Every Day: Little Lessons on Living a Big Life
(Sourcebooks, 2006)

For bulk pricing on any books by David Avrin, contact info@DavidAvrin.com